Choo WaiHong was a corporate lawyer with top law firms in Singapore and California before she took early retirement in 2006 and began writing travel pieces for publications such as *China Daily*. She lived for six years with the Mosuo tribe and now spends half the year with them in Yunnan, China.

THE
KINGDOM
OF
WOMEN

Life, Love and Death in
China's Hidden Mountains

CHOO WAIHONG

I.B. TAURIS
LONDON · NEW YORK

Published in 2017 by
I.B.Tauris & Co. Ltd
London • New York
www.ibtauris.com

ISBN: 978 1 78453 724 1
eISBN: 978 1 78672 170 9
ePDF: 978 1 78673 170 8

A full CIP record for this book is available from the British Library
A full CIP record is available from the Library of Congress

Library of Congress Catalog Card Number: available

Typeset in Perpetua by A. & D. Worthington, Newmarket
Printed and bound in Great Britain by T. J. International, Padstow, Cornwall

To my dearest friend Yvonne Jefferies, litigation solicitor extraordinaire, without whose brilliant suggestion this book would never have been conceived.

And to a special soulmate, the late Margaret Allen, journalist and writer extraordinaire, without whose encouragement and critical eye this book would never have seen the light of day.

Contents

Plates

16. Zhaxi, reputedly the 'Prince of Walking Marriages' or the Don Juan of Don Juans.

Unless stated otherwise, all photographs are the author's own.

Acknowledgements

My first acknowledgement must go to my dearest friend Yvonne Jefferies, who at the end of a visit to my Mosuo home in Lugu Lake suggested that I write about my experiences among the matrilineal Mosuo tribe. With her suggestion came a list of 12 topics she scribbled on the back of an envelope, which formed the basis of the chapter headings of this book. Not only did Yvonne inspire me to embark upon this book but provided a London refuge to complete my manuscript in utter comfort and warmth, for which I shall forever be grateful.

Encouraging me all the way while I was nursing the manuscript was my close friend the late Margaret Allen, herself the author of nearly a dozen books. Margaret used her critical eye as the first reader of my completed work to make invaluable suggestions without which this book would have been the poorer. I only wish she could have seen it through to publication.

When I was struggling with an appropriate and catchy title for the book, my friend Choong Chu, a media consultant, came up with a winning formula – grateful thanks to him.

I am indebted to my editor Tatiana Wilde for her sharp critique which led me on a path of rediscovery that refined many of my previous assumptions and conclusions. The book is in much better shape for her guidance and intelligence.

The wonderful pictures appearing in the book are among the hundreds taken by my favourite photographers, beginning with my brother, photographer Lee Choo, my friends Tjio Kayloe and Tom Jefferies, and professional photographer Aujin Rew. The rustic map of Lugu Lake was designed at short notice by Nathan Chia.

Thanks also go to two friends in China, Ben Mok, with his unreserved support of my social enterprise rice project, and Houston Wu, with his keen perspective on Chinese culture.

I have left the last but not least acknowledgements to my Mosuo friends for so warmly inviting me into their homes and families and sharing their unique world with me. My thanks go especially to Gumi and my godchildren, Ladzu and Nongbu, who have become my Mosuo family. I am grateful for the close friendship extended by Erchima and Zhaxi, Jizuo, Duojie, the late Aha grandmother, Zhiba Zhashi and other Mosuo friends too many to name.

Preface

I never set out to write a book when I first stepped inside the Kingdom of Women. I was on a journey to discover my Chinese roots and explore the vast land of my ancestors with its 5,000 years of historical and cultural treasures. Picturesque Lugu Lake, on the borders of Yunnan and Sichuan in western China, the home of the Mosuo tribe, was just one stop on my grand tour of China.

Tucked away in this remote part of China was a tribal community reputed to be one of the last surviving matrilineal societies in the world. The Mosuo tribe seemed to be frozen in a time and place that had long since died out in China. The fact that it was also matriarchal touched a deep nerve in me, too. (By *matrilineal* I mean tracing a family's descendants and kinship purely through the female bloodline; by *matriarchal* I mean a society that recognizes a woman as the head of the family.)

I didn't know it at the time, but events would occur to spur my return to this place and its people again and again, setting in motion an unplanned extended journey of almost unimaginable adventure. I began my journey as a curious tourist, but over several years I gradually became part of the Mosuo community itself.

I have been a feminist all my life. I grew up with a father who was the quintessential male in an extremely patriarchal Chinese community in Singapore. The nascent feminist in me sharpened over time as I became a corporate lawyer in an intensely male-dominated world.

The Mosuo friends I made in the Kingdom of Women presented me with a wealth of life stories, anecdotes, myths and legends that described a compelling world, so different from the one I knew.

The Mosuo is a culture that celebrates every aspect and stage of womanhood and places the indomitable female spirit at its centre. If there ever had been a feminist utopia, the so-called Kingdom of Women would surely have been it.

The lessons I drew from the Mosuo are lessons for a world that is so often preoccupied with sustaining a patriarchal system that it justifies the suppression of one-half of humankind. The matrilineal and matriarchal principles worked out by Mosuo society can inspire us to envision a better and more equal Brave New World for all of us.

This account of my life with the Mosuo, in a place that has become my spiritual home, has been a labour of love. I only hope that this unique and fragile world will not become a relic of history, as its people transition into modern times.

Prelude

It was a quiet Sunday morning. Coffee in hand, I had settled uncomfortably in the airless, deserted office, trying to catch up on the unanswered emails of the past week and start on the first of five overdue legal opinions.

Having finished the last email, I was taking a breather, looking out of the window at the peaceful Singapore River scene below when the phone rang unusually loudly in the noiseless empty workplace.

'WaiHong, what are you doing at the office?' an excited American voice cried out in surprise on the line. I recognized the caller immediately. Brad was my favourite client, unfailingly polite even in the most tense of moments. Calling me on a Sunday obviously meant he too was busy at work, in his case on a Saturday evening in California, 15 hours behind my timezone.

'Waiting for your phone call!' I said in a tone I hoped sounded more cheerful than I felt. 'What's up?'

'We have a small emergency,' said the legal counsel heading the Asian operations of the world's largest bond fund management house.

'There goes my Sunday catch-up,' I thought to myself, as I took up my pen to jot down my client's latest instructions. We talked through the regulatory issue he was facing and I promised to get back to him by the close of my day. I then spent the rest of that afternoon trying to solve the problem, leaving my unfinished workload, well, unfinished.

Monday followed too quickly, and it was back to the predictable 15-hour-day grind, packed solid with back-to-back meetings, endless client phone calls and a new workload to be farmed out to my team of five lawyers. This day would turn out like every other day in my decades-long legal career, plodding through multiple timezones. The morning hours were dedicated to clients in the Asian timezones, in sync with my own Singapore time. Following a quick lunch break, the afternoon hours would be reserved for clients in Luxembourg and London at the start of their workday. After a fast-food dinner, I would be ready to spend the late-night hours with my clients in the North American timezones from New York to Los Angeles. I would get home around midnight. The routine would begin all over again the next day, and again ...

The interminably long hours were not the only bugbear in my professional life. As the leading light (not my words but those in the fund management business) in my specialized legal field, I had the added pressure of keeping on top of it all. There were conferences to attend, speeches to give, regulators to lobby and countless cocktail parties to attend.

I led a team that earned a tidy sum from our billings, yet I was constantly encouraged to increase those billings by 30 per cent annually. There just weren't enough hours in a day.

As a partner initially in the largest law firm in the country and then in the world, I had to keep up with the internal politicking that riddled all large corporate establishments. A lot of that had to do with being part of the boys' club and playing by their rules. The point was that as a woman, I never really belonged. I also never took the time to under-stand the rules that were intuitively understood by the men.

I voiced my opinions as and when they made sense to me. What guided me were ideas such as fairness, non-discrimination and funda-mental rights in the workplace, quite useless markers in hindsight. I was blind to what was required to climb the ladder to the top.

I have lost count of the times I 'misspoke' at partners' meetings. There was the time I objected to a proposal to reduce the period of maternity leave for women partners. I won. During the annual recruit-ment exercise, I would be the lone voice reminding the male partners to base their choices on the merits of female applicants as they did for male applicants instead of on their comeliness.

That said, my bank balance was in a healthy state. I had a home so stylishly modern that it was featured in *Prestige*, a fancy lifestyle maga-zine. Now and then I would make it to the society pages. For leisure, I zoomed around in my Porsche convertible on weekend jaunts and jetted off to fashionable cities around the world. I treated myself to more Michelin three-star restaurants than I could count – or needed.

What did it all amount to, I found myself asking on that fateful Sunday afternoon at work. Was it all worth it? Could it get any better? Had I been too long in this demanding profession?

It had not been an easy ride for a single woman professional like me. Unlike the boys in the club, I had no spousal support at home to whom I could delegate the small domestic things in life. No one kept house and the refrigerator stocked for me. I single-handedly did all the big and small things in order to play at being a top-notch corporate lawyer in the dog-eat-dog world of modern finance.

Being a lawyer so filled my life that I had no other. I had no family life, no significant other, no kids, nothing really to look back on with a smile.

If I continued with the life I had, nothing would change. However hard I looked, I knew there was no light at the end of the tunnel. That realization came upon me as I watched the sun set over the Singapore River in that epiphanic moment on that fateful Sunday evening. I was convinced that life would not get any better from then on.

A small voice whispered softly into my inner ear. It was time to move on. On to what, I had no idea. Only that anything was better than this endless mad turning of the wheel in the hamster cage.

In that rare moment of inspiration, I drafted a letter of resignation. It was a simple draft, saying that I was quitting for personal reasons. Writing it was the easy part, delivering it the difficult bit. I developed cold feet thinking about it. How would I face the partners with this note? How would I explain what I really felt in my heart of hearts?

At the end, I chose the easy way out. I clicked on the keyboard and emailed it across to my immediate boss just before switching off the lights in the office. The deed was done.

My boss was kind enough to call me almost immediately. We talked for a while and when he heard the resolution in my voice, he proffered what would turn out to be excellent advice.

'Rewrite your letter. Don't say "personal" reasons, as that has negative connotations. Say "family" reasons. It would go down better.'

What did I know? There I was, goofing it up again, not understanding the nuances only those in the mysterious exclusive club understood. It was just as well I was leaving it all behind. I was never a part of it anyway.

To say that I went home that night and opened a bottle of '85 Churchill champagne would be a lie. However, as I stepped through the door at home, I felt a sudden lightness of being, as if the whole burden of my former life had been lifted. I was free. I could sleep in tomorrow and never have to hurry out the door again. I could have brunch instead of breakfast. I could do that every day from then on. I did not have to make plans for every minute of the next day, and the next. I could turn a new page. I could spend the rest of my life going where whim and fancy would take me.

I was done with my former life. I was packing it in. I was leaving for untold adventures.

Towards Tibet

CHINA

BEIJING

SHANGHAI

LIJIANG

KINGDOM OF WOMEN

1	Xienami Mother Lake (Lugu Lake)
2	Musuo pig trough boat
3	Moon Lake
4	Gemu Mountain Goddess
5	My Cottage by Moon Lake
6	My four-wheel drive
7	Gemu Shrine
8	My Godchildren's home hearth
9	Yongning Town
10	Zhameisi Temple Complex
11	Circle dance round a bonfire
12	Airport for Lugu Lake

LEGEND

〜〜〜 Main Road Access   ﹏﹏﹏ 18-Bend Road to Lijiang

· · · · · · · Mud Track   ▶ Directional Signs

*MAP NOT DRAWN TO SCALE

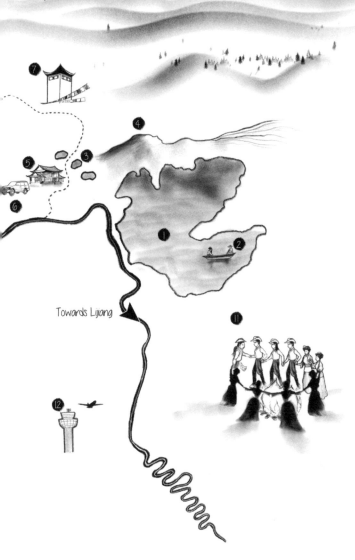

KINGDOM OF WOMEN

Towards Lijiang

1

Arriving in the Kingdom of Women

Once in a blue moon, a traveller may be lucky enough to come across the mention of a place so intriguing, so mysterious, that not to answer its call would be unforgivable. It was months since I had quit my job. Following my urge to discover what China would hold for me, I had spent my time travelling to the more widely known cities and countryside of this vast country of my ancestors. Then I came across an article in a travel magazine about a remote tribe in a corner of Yunnan where the people worshipped a mountain goddess called Gemu.

This tribe, located by a lake in the far eastern foothills of the great Himalayan range, apparently was one of the few surviving matrilineal societies in the world. It struck me as incredible that a matrilineal society still existed in the twenty-first century, let alone in the depths of patriarchal China. This is the land where patriarchy is so deep-rooted that a male-biased mentality has, mainly through abortion, produced a skewed gender imbalance of nearly 120 boys born to every 100 girls today. This is also the place from which my grandfather fled to escape poverty and start a new life in Malaysia. There he planted his traditional patriarchal roots, which produced in my father an intransigent preference for boys and which in turn produced in me a stubborn advocacy for fair and equal treatment of women in a man's world.

To say that the feminist heart in me was beating a little faster on reading that this Mosuo tribe practises a religious ceremony celebrating a female deity would be an understatement. Even the name given to this tribe by the Chinese, the Kingdom of Women, conjures up an unimaginable world populated by present-day Amazons.

I was curious to find out just how the story of the Mosuo tribe came about. Equipped with only a limited mastery of the Chinese language, I trawled through books and articles written by anthropologists, historians, journalists and sociologists, and pieced together an introduction to the story of the Kingdom of Women.

A couple of thousand years ago, or even longer depending on which book you read, the Mosuos, originally known as the Na people, walked from the high mountains in the north-west to where they are today, in search of a kinder climate. They must have trekked for years and years, passing over countless harsh mountain ranges before coming across a great plateau situated in a lower altitude, much more hospitable than their previous homeland.

There they eyed a beautiful lake under the shade of a high granite mountain. By its shore, they found the weather warmer, the spring water clearer, the soil richer and the pine forests with wild animals and plant life more abundant. Their discovery led them to settle down among the knolls and valleys studded around the Yongning plateau by the lake. They claimed the lake as their own and graced its life-giving waters with a name recalling the greatest female force, that of the Mother Lake, or Xienami. The lake was renamed later as Lugu Lake because it is shaped like a 'lugu', a water container made from the dried shell of a gourd. More significantly, they claimed the mountain as their own, acknowledging it also as female, in the form of a new beautiful goddess and protectrix, Gemu.

The Na people brought with them their old way of life, gathering forest produce, hunting animals big and small and planting rudimentary crops on their small homesteads. They also brought along with them something precious from the past, a past so remote that some historians say it was as old as the dawn of human history. This precious relic harks back to a time when the world was full of deities representing the many faces of nature, the main ones almost always wearing a female face. Modern scholars may label them merely as fertility goddesses but they formed the spiritual bedrock of human society then.

This spirit of embracing the female as the building block of society, represented by Gemu Mountain Goddess, was the jewel in the crown brought by the Na to the Mother Lake. As they began building up their new lives, they re-organized their community along the well-worn path adopted by their foremothers, that of creating and linking family members by their matrilineal bloodline. They built large homes with pine logs cut from the mountainside to house their female-descended families, taking pains to stay connected to the primal maternal thread.

The puzzle of how the Mosuos came to be what they are may never be solved definitively, but if I may borrow from the school of thought that suggests that all humankind started out as matrilineal societies, I would venture to say that the history of the Mosuos must have dated back to the beginning of the human epoch tens of thousands of years ago.

That the Mosuos have been strictly matrilineal over time is not in doubt. That they worship the forces of nature just as our forebears did in early pagan societies is also evident. That they revere most of all Gemu, a female mountain goddess, among the many deities they hold dear, harkens back to the oldest human tradition of worshipping the Great Goddess and other lesser goddesses in the Old Stone Age of human existence.

Archeologists have uncovered many instances of ancient goddess worship throughout the world. There was the original Great Goddess, the Mother Goddess, there was the Goddess Hera in Greece, the female deity Isis in Egypt, Parvati the Goddess in southern India, even Berehinia, the Mother Goddess of Russia. China had her own Great Goddess, Nu-Wa. Following these female-centric traditions, perhaps the Mosuos can claim an unbroken direct link to those early days of human society. And just maybe they can further claim to be one of the few remnants of the original matrilineal human society.

The real puzzle is how the Mosuo tribe has managed to cling tenaciously to that ancient matrilineal tradition without succumbing to later paternalistic influences all around them.

Compare the Mosuos on the western side of Lugu Lake who to this day remain staunchly matrilineal, to their cousins on the eastern side of the lake who have become patrilineal over time. The eastern Mosuos chose to adopt the paternalistic alternative, having paired up with Mongolian troops who remained behind after Kublai Khan annexed Yunnan to China in the thirteenth century. The Mongols brought with them their male-centred way of life to the eastern Mosuo community, who so identified themselves with being the descendants of Mongols that in recent times they had successfully petitioned to classify themselves as belonging to the 'Mongol' minority tribe, not the Mosuo tribe. But despite the patriarchal conversion of their eastern cousins, the western Mosuos remain untouched by male-centric influences.

It was not just against the influence of their immediate Mosuo cousins that the tribe held fast to its matrilineal heritage. Against all odds, the tribe kept its matrilineage despite coming into contact with other neighbouring mountain tribes that venerated male gods and followed a patriarchal tradition.

More tellingly, the Mosuos have so far been able to withstand the pressures brought about by the male-dominated Chinese culture that took root 5,000 years ago and spread throughout China. Han Chinese patriarchy is intense and all pervasive, continuing to hold sway even in contemporary China. Born and bred in the same cultural milieu adopted by a largely Chinese immigrant society in Singapore, I too am familiar with navigating a world where men are the bosses both at home and outside, and where women find themselves relegated to a place in the family way behind their husbands and sons. Things may have improved for women since they entered the workforce at all levels in this century, but, for all that, patriarchy remains omnipresent in Chinese society.

To me the story of a people who pay homage to a goddess in a world full of father figures as godheads and follow a matriarchal way of life in a world where patriarchy rules is so interesting and entirely unique that it seems too good to be true. I felt the need to get up close to a real goddess waiting to be seen and touched. I wanted to see for myself just how this tribe manages to exist as a feminist oddity in patriarchal China.

Dropping all my other travel plans, I made straight for Lugu Lake, set in the remote south-westernmost province of Yunnan in China. As luck would have it, I timed my visit to coincide with the Mountain Goddess Festival held every summer in honour of Gemu. The festival is known locally as Zhuanshanjie, or 'Perambulating Round the Mountain' in Chinese, and is the most important festival of the Mosuo people.

Gemu the mountain deity is a giant granite mountain sitting 3,600 metres astride Lugu Lake situated deep inside high mountains. Had I travelled there 90 years ago, as did the Austrian botanist-explorer and writer Joseph Rock, it would have taken me seven days to ride horseback from the nearest old tea-trade centre of Lijiang over an ancient mountain trail across nearly 200 kilometres of rough terrain. As it turned out, I set off from Lijiang in the comfort of a chauffeur-driven car speeding on a modern, winding tarmac road.

The drive was scenic although arduous as we wound our way up and down the mountainous route. This was pine-studded countryside with spectacular vistas of snowy mountain peaks and small valleys washed by the Jinshajiang, the Golden Sand River, the first tributary of China's great Yangtze River. The going was not easy, as the narrow two-way single-lane road was perched precariously over steep mountainsides with frequent traffic jams caused not so much by cars as herds of mountain goats and cows ignoring the traffic in search of green pastures on the other side.

At the end of a gruelling seven-hour journey, the car ascended a final crest and, turning round a curve of the road, revealed a picture-postcard view of a majestic blue lake. That first sight of Lugu Lake, no matter how many return trips I make, never fails to take my breath away. Nestled within ring upon concentric ring of mountain ranges, the large lake has a beautiful serpentine shoreline punctuated with hundreds of tiny isthmuses, studded with endless rows of Christmas pine trees dipping right by the clear water's edge.

On the day of my arrival under a clear blue, cloudless sky, the lake reflected an intense azure blue, the bluest blue I had ever seen. On a nasty day, with rain-soaked clouds hanging overhead, Lugu Lake turns a moody slate-blue hue. On a crisp cold winter's day with the sun shining brightly, the lake transforms itself into a bright emerald green body of water.

As I gazed from the lake to the horizon, a tall stone sierra sat majestically across the entire length of the shoreline on the far side. Oddly, the montane structure bore a distinct shape. Squinting my eyes, I focused on the massif taking on the shape of a human-like figure, the outline of which looked just like a reclining woman in profile, a forehead rising to an aquiline nose ending in an elegant chin, framed with a gentle cascade of long hair flowing down the summit head. The profile traced the chin down to a beautiful neck that rose towards an upturned generous bosom before sliding into a slight hint of a tummy, with the rest of the reclining body trailing down like a long graceful skirt. The entire picture bore an uncanny resemblance to a female form in repose.

'There she is, Gemu Mountain Goddess!' my driver chipped in to give voice to my unspoken thoughts.

So I had finally come face to face with the lady mountain deity. This unique female demiurge would be the object of special worship by the Mosuo tribe at the Gemu Mountain Goddess Festival the following day.

On the day of the festival, I rose early to a wet morning, the summer rains having arrived with a vengeance overnight. I waded through puddles to my driver in the waiting car. Making our way to the site of the festival, we swished over a muddy wet track hacked from the side of the mountain meant more for horses than cars. We bumped over squelchy potholes as we drove on until we ran right into a mighty big one. Revving hard, the driver got stuck deeper and deeper, spraying wet mud all over the place. Mercifully a couple of passers-by kindly came forward to help out, and somehow with the help of a few boulders and planks thrown in the path of the wheels, they managed to push us out of the pothole and send us on our way.

Before long, I saw in front of me crowds of people scurrying up a hillside, with more arriving by horseback and motorbikes. We had arrived just in time to witness the start of the festivities.

Unfolding before me was a lively scene. Locals dressed in their ethnic finest were busy pitching makeshift tents, tending to open fires, watching over pots of steaming rice and boiling broths, flitting about chatting with old friends and relatives. Children screeched with delight as they played catch with each other. In pole position sat a huge tent housing a group of Tibetan Buddhist lamas, the keepers of the faith, with two of their number blowing long alpine horns to herald the start of the festival.

A stream of worshippers trekked slowly up the slope towards a small simple white shrine built on a rise up on the northern face of Gemu Mountain. I trailed them to the worship site and watched the throng of women and men going through their paces as they paid homage to their mountain goddess.

'How do you do this?' I asked a friendly face.

'You first light incense and pine branches,' she said, handing some to me, 'and put them in front of the shrine. This is to get Gemu's attention.'

I followed her instructions. Then she beckoned me to follow her up the few steps to stand before the shrine.

'Just do what I do,' she said.

She put her palms together in the universal prayer mode, then positioned them first to her forehead, then her mouth and finally next to her heart before getting on her knees. In a half-prostrate pose, she opened her palms and placed each on the floor on either side of her and lowered her head to place it on the ground. She got up again and repeated the ritual two more times. After the third prostration, she got up and with palms pressed together in front of her face mouthed a silent prayer with her eyes closed.

She waited for me as I went through the paces, and indicated to me that I should follow her as she began her pilgrim's circumambulation round the shrine three times. This was done in a clockwise direction as she continued to mumble her prayers quietly.

Lastly, she unstrung a length of Tibetan-style prayer streamers and tied both ends up on tree branches by the side of the shrine in order for the wind to hurry her prayers to the goddess.

'I prayed for Gemu to be happy and also to bless my family with another year of plentiful harvest and good health,' she explained later when I asked her to tell me about her prayers.

After thanking her, I followed the crowd down the slope to mill around the merry-makers. People gathered around a patch of green to wait for the start of the entertainment. A Mosuo man strode centre stage and lifted his flute to his lips. Softly he blew a soulful tune which I was later to learn was the usual signal for the start of the circle dance. A few brave souls stepped forward eagerly to link their hands and began moving to the rhythm of the flautist's music and gait as he led them round the makeshift dance floor.

Soon more locals joined in, hurrying to assume their positions in the dance line, the men in front, the women following and the children trailing behind. And dressed up they all were, the women resplendent in their colourful headdresses matching their multi-hued tops, swishing their long flowing white skirts, with the men jaunty under cowboy hats in their bright yellow tops. Everyone joined hands to form a dancing circle behind the piper as he continued with his four-beat tune. Keeping beat, the men stomped in their high boots, the women danced grace-fully and the children struggled to keep up. Now and then the dancing troupe broke out in loud chorus, singing to the familiar tune.

As the dancing continued, the onlookers made their way to their tents for an afternoon of feasting and wining. I too went in search of lunch and struck lucky when I stepped into the tent where a large family had congregated. In the crowded tent an elderly woman held court, surrounded by her many children and grandchildren. I smiled, and offered the woman a pack of cigarettes. She motioned me to sit next to her. Looking around, I spied a not-so-shy granddaughter and began engaging her in conversation. The teenage girl with a winning smile was called Cher-er Ladzu.

'What is this festival all about?' I asked Ladzu.

'Today is Zhuanshanjie and we come here to celebrate the day dedicated to Gemu Mountain Goddess. I have been looking forward to this all year,' she told me.

As I settled in hoping for an invitation to the family picnic meal, Ladzu's grandmother chipped in:

'Gemu is our protector. Her duty is to look after all the Mosuo people by the lake. We give thanks to the goddess on her big day which falls on the 25th day of the seventh moon in the lunar year.'

Her next words, 'Would you like to share our meal with us?', were music to my ears. Lunch, she gestured to the boiling pot outside the tent, was a whole piglet cooked slowly in a soup. We tucked into the delicious meat with our fingers, picnic style. Someone offered me a choice of hot tea, beer or home-brewed *kwangtan* rice wine and I sat with Ladzu's family, sipping and people-watching the afternoon away.

A festival always opens a window to the soul of the community that celebrates it. To me the Mosuo tribe's keeping the Mountain Goddess Festival alive suggests a couple of things. Worshipping a mountain deity is part and parcel of the worship of nature, harking back to an ancient pagan tradition. Early humans venerated nature in one form or another, and deified objects such as the sky, the sun, the moon, streams, rock formations, animals and, not least, mountains. The Mosuos are no different and in continuing to celebrate and worship this mountain deity of theirs, they tell us that far from abandoning their ancient beliefs, they set great store in being connected to their cultural and religious origins.

In choosing to celebrate Gemu, a goddess instead of a god, the Mosuos also recognize the position of the female in their world. Here is the link between the Mosuo choice of a goddess, not a god, and the matrilineal heritage of this particular tribe. The choice of the female Gemu as their most important deity tells us that this community upholds femaleness as the cardinal principle at its heart and soul. It is consistent with their core value of tracing their lineage through the matrilineal bloodline.

These stubborn feminists, both women and men, return annually to Gemu's shrine on the holy mountain to remind themselves of the place of the female in their universe. They are superstitious enough to pay homage to their divine protectrix to make sure that things turn out well for them in the coming year. The quality of their lives, they believe, depends on Gemu's largesse. Her job, after all, is to bless and protect the Mosuo people who live under her shadow.

Besides observing the ancient ritual of worshipping Gemu Mountain Goddess, the Mosuos, I would come to learn, hold dear many other age-old cultural customs that are different and unique to them. One of my favourite stories is about how a Mosuo life is a dog's life, literally. Not in the sense of a miserable life as the phrase is used generally, but in a deep sense of gratitude to the dog, the one animal that made the ultimate sacrifice of exchanging a long life in favour of humans. The lovely story of the dog and its special place in the Mosuo world is told time and again to every Mosuo child, and I would paraphrase it from the words of a Mosuo friend when I asked her about it.

'Once upon a long, long time ago, the Great Spirit decided to dole out different lifespans to all the creatures under the sun. The rule of the game is to be the first animal to respond to the Great Spirit's calling out a number to represent a certain lifespan.

'"A thousand years!" the Great Spirit called out for the first time at the crack of dawn. An early riser, the wild goose flying overhead, squawked its claim to the thousand-year lifespan.

11

'"One hundred years!" the Great Spirit made his second call. Flying behind the wild goose, a duck swooped down to lay claim on that second-best lifespan.

'And so the calls went on and on, the lifespans decreasing in descending order.

'"Sixty years!" was one of the final calls. Already up and wagging its tail, the dog took up that offer.

'"13 years!" was the last call made late in the morning. The tardy Mosuo who finally woke up had no choice but to put her hand up. On behalf of humans, she drew the shortest straw on offer.

'Greedy human nature being what it is, the Mosuo claimant expressed how disappointed she was with humans being granted such a short lifespan. "We want more!" she pleaded with the Great Spirit.

'"Ask some other creature to swap its lifespan with you," came the reply.

'So she tried, making the rounds from the goose to every other animal down the line. All of them refused to budge. Finally, she reached the friendly ears of the dog.

'"How about it? My 13 years for your 60?" the human representative pleaded with the dog. The dog tilted its head, pondered for a moment before its generous nature took over.

'"All right, 13 years is long enough if I lead a happy life. Feed me three times a day and never beat me, and I will swap my lifespan with yours!"

'With that, the deal was done. From that day, humans lived their lives to the ripe old age of 60 years, while the dog lived a shorter but pampered life of 13 years.'

To honour their side of the bargain, the Mosuos came to value their canine donor and to this day live up to the promise of treating the dog as their benefactor. They are exceptionally kind to their dogs, not in the overindulgent way dogs are treated as pets but certainly in a much more special way than other domesticated animals. Every child is taught to be tender and kind to the dog and I do not know any local who knowingly abuses or abandons one. A Mosuo always makes sure the family dog is fed at family meal times. More than once I have witnessed a Mosuo turning up her nose and shaking her head should there be a mention of the 'delicacy' of dog meat being served in a Chinese restaurant.

The timeworn story of the Mosuo and her dog is brought to life whenever a child in a family reaches puberty in her 13th year. Each Mosuo family marks the crossing of this threshold by enacting a coming-of-age ceremony. It signifies the child's entry into adulthood and is unique, in that reaching puberty is not celebrated in contemporary Chinese culture.

What is more unusual is how the Mosuos link it back to their beloved dog story. The choice of the 13th year as the point of transition into adulthood coincides exactly with the lifespan originally allocated to humans but eventually swapped with the dog. It is in remembrance of their life-long debt to the dog for its special gift that the Mosuos remind the new adult in their family to feed the family dog with a special big meal at the end of the ceremony.

When a family holds the ceremony, it takes place on the first day of the Lunar New Year in the Chinese calendar. The occasion does not occur on the child's 13th birthday, as one might expect. The Mosuos do not count the birth date of a person to mark her age. Her age is counted by reference to each passing Lunar New Year Day. In the old days before the lunar calendar was adopted, her forebears would have counted her age when spring came along – another spring, another year.

The family with a teenager soon to be 13 years old prepares for the special day well in advance of the big event. The house is spring-cleaned, new clothing is bought for the teenager and much food is prepared for the big party to which every family in the village is invited.

I had to arrive at the crack of dawn to attend my first such event held at the home of a Mosuo family who owned a lodge in the lakeside hamlet of Lige and would later become my close friends. Squeezing in among the crowd of relatives and curious tourists already gathered there in front of a burning fire by the hearth, I turned to ask a local next to me about the significance of the ceremony.

'To us Mosuos, the coming of age at 13 years is the biggest day of our lives. We call it the "Becoming an Adult Celebration",' she said.

The name of the young girl being honoured on that day was Xiao Wujing (or 'Little Five-Pounder', on account of her weight at birth), the daughter of the lodge owners. All eyes were set upon Wujing as she made her appearance into the family room. This was an event she would have been looking forward to for the longest time. That day marked the 13th spring from the year she was born, and was the most significant day in her young life – the day she came of age. On becoming an adult from that moment on, Wujing would be a fully fledged person on whom would be conferred all the attendant rights of a grown-up.

As an adult she would be entitled to wear the full Mosuo dress, something that she was not allowed to do beforehand. Putting on the dress would thus be the principal symbolic act of the ceremony.

Little Five-Pounder, dressed in an everyday track-suit ensemble like any other teenager, looked a little nervous as she walked over to the 'female' log pillar on the left side of the room (see p. 26 for an explanation of gendered pillars).

Someone led her over to stand with one foot on a big bag of rice while the other foot was placed on a dry-cured whole pig, a symbol of wealth to the Mosuos. The rice signified an adult life blessed with ample food on the table and the pig with bounteous fecundity.

The eldest maternal aunt of Wujing had the honour of conducting the ceremony of the 'Wearing of the Skirt'. The aunt began by holding a long, white, pleated skirt for the girl to step into before tying it around her still tiny waist. Then she helped the girl into a bright red jacket, cinching it with a bright pink sash around her middle. For the finishing touch, the aunt placed the traditional decorative braided headdress on the girl's head. Suddenly Little Five-Pounder was transformed from a tomboy in sporting gear to a fully dressed-up young Mosuo woman.

Continuing with the ritual, the aunt chanted in the Mosuo language.

'Today you are matured as a person. I wish you a long, smooth life with few problems. Go forth into your adult life, for now you know how to conduct yourself properly.'

Looking a bit bewildered, Little Five-Pounder looked up and nodded, her eyes revealing that she understood the solemnity of the occasion.

Her adulthood having been witnessed by her entire family and the entire village, Wujing gave thanks by prostrating herself three times before each of her elders, first to her aunt, then to her mother and everyone else. Steamy yak butter tea was served all around to mark the end of the formal ritual while Wujing stole away to present a special big meal to the family dog.

Soon after, we were all ushered outside into the courtyard to join in a big feast. Every household in the community was invited to the celebration, and, as is local custom, at least one representative per household was there to bear witness to the occasion and to recognize the new adult as a full member of their community.

I came to understand that coming of age at puberty for a Mosuo person is more than wearing adult clothes. Before the ritual, a Mosuo child would have been considered not so much a non-person as a 'yet-to-be-recognized' person in the community. If a child should die before becoming an adult, she would not be entitled to a full and proper funeral rite. On becoming a person in the 13th spring of her life, she could look forward to a long life as part of her matrilineal family and a member of the larger community.

Fast forward a couple of years and I was given the chance to take a more active role in another 'Becoming an Adult' ceremony. On that occasion, Nongbu, the younger brother of Ladzu, was turning 13. The parents of the youngster had come to me with a strange request when I arrived at their home.

'Can you conduct the "Wearing the Trousers" ritual for our boy?'

'Er, is this similar to the "Wearing the Skirt" thing for girls? I am not really sure how to do this. Why don't you do it?'

'We are also not sure how to do it!'

I gave in, instinctively realizing that an honour was being presented to me and was something I could not refuse. Going purely by my recall of what I had seen at Little Five-Pounder's coming-of-age event, I pretended I knew what to do.

'Is there a male pillar in the room?' I asked.

'Here, on the right, where I have placed the rice and dried whole pig,' Nongbu's mother replied.

I led the boy still dressed in a jumper and jeans to the correct gender pillar and got him in position on top of the two symbolic temporary footstools. His mother handed me a large pair of trousers. I held them before the boy and motioned to him to step in. With that, he wore his first pair of grown-up trousers.

Prompting me on, his mother gave me a long Tibetan-style jacket, much too big for the still undeveloped 13-year-old. I managed to get his arms into the long sleeves but got into trouble when I tried to tie the bulky thing around his tiny frame. Nongbu's maternal aunt quickly stepped in to give a hand. Fully attired in adult clothes, Nongbu waited for the final touch, which I quickly supplied by placing a furry hunter's hat on his small head.

Then came the moment for me to say something special to give meaning to the ritual. I improvised.

'Nongbu, you are now a man. Remember to always do the right thing, and never forget to look after your family,' I said softly, hoping that the words sufficed.

For this young man, becoming an adult meant he would be gradually inducted into the role of the Mosuo male. Among other things, he would be expected to contribute his physical strength to the manual chores around the family farm while continuing to live among his maternal relatives for life. He would be free to form a relationship with any woman he chose but would not marry the *axia*, a 'lover' in the Mosuo language, nor bring her home because the home comprised members of his matrilineal family only. He also had no responsibility or claim over any offspring that his *axia* might give birth to, as that baby will belong to his *axia*'s family, not his. No husbandly or fatherly duties for him.

For a young woman such as Wujing, she gets an extra perk on reaching adulthood, her very own room at her maternal home. She too is given a free hand to live and love in her maternal home, where she will cohabit with her siblings, her maternal cousins, her mother, her maternal aunts and uncles and her maternal grandmother, an arrangement which will last a lifetime. She is at liberty to practise the 'walking marriage' way of Mosuo love life, choosing her *axias* without ever having to marry any of them or move away to his home or indeed to form a family of her own with him. As she grows older, she will be encouraged to bear children to add to her matrilineal family. Any child born to her will belong solely to her matrilineal family.

None of these unique social arrangements practised by the Mosuos exist anywhere else in China, whether in historical or modern times. Probably none of them exist anywhere else in the rest of the world today. None of them could ever exist in any male-dominant society that is the antithesis of matriarchy.

Through the labyrinthine mix of folktales and legends of their pagan past overlaid by their Tibetan Buddhist present, the Mosuos hang on to one preponderant unbroken thread, that of the celebration of the female. While the moon is considered a female force of nature in most cultures, with the Mosuo culture also venerating it as a goddess, the sun is usually seen as a male deity in many ancient cultures. In the Mosuo spiritual world, the sun is a goddess, irrefutably female. To this matriarchal tribe, mountain deities can either be female goddesses or male gods, but the most adored of them all is a female, Gemu the Mountain Goddess. This is the very reason that drew the feminist in me to Lugu Lake in the first place. As I left the festival, a fleeting thought flashed through my mind. Right here in China's hidden mountains lies the promise of the most intriguing story about women.

2

Building a Mosuo Home

My first foray to Lugu Lake was a fleeting tourist stop, pleasant enough to jot down my wanderings on a couple of postcards home. Through a series of unexpected but pleasant twists of fate, my second visit committed me to building a cottage right under the shadow of Gemu Goddess Mountain. By my fifth visit, I moved into a new Mosuo home nestled in a circle of pine-studded knolls. This is no run-of-the-mill story of how I came to be an habitué in the Kingdom of Women.

On my very first visit, I booked myself into a rustic waterfront room in a guesthouse by the lake and took in the sights and sounds of this charming mountain hideaway a million miles from the madding crowds of urban China. I feasted my eyes on the picturesque semi-alpine scenery, rode the cable car to the top of the Goddess Mountain, supped on Chinese barbeques and drank the local rice wine. I made cursory conversations with passing tourists after watching the nightly Mosuo dance performed around a bonfire. All in all an interesting stop in my peripatetic itinerary around China.

On my second visit the following spring to fulfil a promise to see my goddaughter Ladzu (whom I had first met at the annual Gemu Festival) for the Lunar New Year, I happened to mention her to a local I met on the tour bus to Lugu Lake.

'She is my niece!' exclaimed the big handsome hulk of a man with shoulder-length hair framing his face.

'Ladzu's mother is my younger sister,' added Zhaxi. 'Since you are going to visit her, why don't you stay at the guesthouse I run in the Lige peninsula by the lake?'

And so I decamped to Zhaxi Guesthouse, a homely little delight on a piece of lakeside paradise.

'I will be happy to drive you over to visit Gumi's house over the mountain,' he said the next day.

Meeting Zhaxi paved the way towards my gradual introduction to Gumi's large family of eight siblings who in time would become my extended family in the Kingdom of Women. But I am getting ahead of the story.

True to his word, Zhaxi was kind enough to take me to Gumi's home, where I got re-acquainted with Gumi and my godchildren, and met Gumi's and Zhaxi's mother, a 70-something matriarch of the family. I spent a wonderful day hanging out with the family. A chicken was sacrificed in my honour as we had our lunch on tiny stools by the home hearth.

In those days, Zhaxi held court nightly at his guesthouse, conducting a story-telling session by a coal fire in the middle of his restaurant, spinning yarns and mesmerizing his retinue of Chinese tourists all eager to lap up his endless anecdotes and stories about the Mosuos. I too was one of those spellbound by the tales of a society without marriage, where women were free to choose their partners and men were freed from the constraints of husbandhood and fatherhood. I was unaware that Zhaxi had by then become a legendary one-man band trumpeting the touristy delights of Lugu Lake and the Kingdom of Women. So famous was he on the Chinese internet that scores of travellers literally formed queues on a daily basis to take selfies with him.

A less well-known fact about this inimitable Mosuo character is his love of architecture and building. Besides building the first ever guest-house in Lige, he had built a horse farm right behind the Gemu Mountain. He even orchestrated the building of a grand teahouse on the outskirts of Kunming, the capital city of Yunnan province. By the time we met, he was itching to put his true calling to another test.

'Would you like to have a house built here?' he asked me out of the blue when he hosted a tea party at his horse farm for our motley crew of tourists on a cold January morning, the day after visiting my godchildren.

'What? Here, on this horse farm?' I replied, surprised by this preposterous idea.

'Yes, right here, in this beautiful setting in front of the tiny Moon Lake down there. It can be a simple cottage done in the local style. It won't cost much,' he said.

'How much is not much?' I asked, more out of curiosity than taking his bait.

He suggested a sum that seemed piddling and certainly unbelievable compared to the house prices I was accustomed to in land-scarce Singapore. Why, it would cost much less than buying a new car at home!

'Hmm, I'll think about it,' I said, not committing myself, although I sensed a seed had already been planted there and then.

Meanwhile, back in my densely populated hometown of Singapore, I brooded over this incredible proposition. As I took my evening walks breathing in the gas fumes along crowded pedestrian sidewalks, the alternate thought of hiking from a cottage nestled in a pine forest round a lake and taking in clean, crisp mountain air seemed more and more inviting. It did not take me long to warm to the idea.

Eagerly I returned to Lige two months later and delivered a very short message to Zhaxi the builder.

'Let's build me that simple and cheap house you mentioned.'

He beamed.

'I have but a few requirements,' I added. 'The house has to look and feel like a local house because I love the look of Mosuo architecture. I want modern sanitation. Most important of all, I want a sitting room just like the all-purpose grandmother's room built around a hearth which I see in every local home.'

That was it – two minutes' worth of specifications for the house to be built on his horse farm. Zhaxi continued to nod his head but did not bother to ask any more questions. It looked as if the deal was on.

Not long after that fateful conversation, I left Lugu Lake, trusting that something would be put in motion. Honestly, I did not know what to expect. Would Zhaxi really start work on the house? When would he begin? Would I have to go back and forth to supervise the construction? A thousand questions came to mind. But I was busy and in the end decided simply to let things happen, if they did at all. What the heck, I thought philosophically, even if nothing came of it, it would only be a small gamble that did not pay off.

In the course of the next few months, I made occasional phone calls to Zhaxi to ask how things were progressing. Mostly I received vague and non-committal answers.

'Yes, I have started,' he said once, without elaborating.

'It's progressing,' he said another time.

'It is going to be the poshest villa in all of Lugu Lake,' he boasted during the next call but did not add much more.

I did not press for more, resigned to the fact that I could only take telephone conversations so far. I would simply rely on blind faith.

Time wore on, and after a while curiosity got the better of me. Four months later, I thought it was high time I paid a site visit to check things out. I set out on foot early in the morning to the horse farm on a familiar hiking route to the Gemu shrine. Leaving Lige and the blue waters of Lugu Lake behind, I trekked up a rocky incline, cutting through the high ground via a winding path to get behind the Goddess Mountain.

As I rounded the small body of water called the Moon Lake, I saw a commotion ahead on a bluff at the horse farm. My heart skipped a beat. I did not know what to expect. As I got nearer, Zhaxi walked from a large group of people to greet me. About 30 Mosuo women and men, some of whom I recognized as his relatives and friends, were gathered to help put up the house structure.

Raising a Mosuo house structure is both a momentous event and a monumental effort requiring as many pairs of hands as one can marshal, as Zhaxi had done. The rugged group he assembled milled about, ready to flex their muscles in a show of community spirit.

They stood beside several large structures lying on the ground. These were huge assembled pieces of log and wood beams connected with crossbeams forming the framework of each wall of the house. There were five such frameworks for my house-to-be, making five sets of walls to be erected that day. I could see that they were tall two-tier structures. The house would be two-storeyed, I thought. When pulled upright and connected perpendicularly with more crossbeams, the five panels would form the inner and outer skeleton of the house, to be bricked in later to complete the walls.

The men were called to order to mount what would turn out to be a giant life-size Lego building set. With one set of ropes, a few of the men tied up the top crossbeams of the first wall framework and carried it next to the foundation stone platform, placing the bases of the beams against corresponding stone plinths. Holding the ends of the ropes, they positioned themselves a few metres away on the platform, ready to pull. Others stationed themselves on the other side of the framework, some with long wooden poles in hand, ready to push.

'Are we ready?' Zhaxi's voice rang out.

Everyone readied himself for the joint endeavour.

'Der, Nye, Suo!'

On the 'Three' of the first shout of 'One, Two, Three', in Mosuo, the pullers pulled in unison. They managed to raise the framework a little. Another shout, 'Der, Nye, Suo', and it was raised yet a little more. By this time the framework was tilted up with enough room on the other side. The pushers got in position behind the columns of the structure, some using strong hands and others planting wooden poles against the columns in order to push the structure up from the opposite side to the pullers.

On the next 'One, Two Three', the pullers and the pushers pulled and pushed, raising the structure higher. On and on the pull-cum-push kept going on the count for another dozen times before the whole framework stood erect. Not letting go yet, the pullers kept the ropes taut and the pushers held up the standing structure while two men rushed off to fetch two holding logs to prop it up. Only then did the pullers and the pushers let up. One structure up, four more to go.

With an economy of tools, someone untied the same set of ropes and used them to truss the next wall framework. The process began all over again for the second wall skeleton. The shouting resumed, as did the pulling and the pushing until the second mount was erected.

With the two wall frameworks standing erect, it was time to connect them Lego-like. The crossbeams fabricated within the framework in one piece were cleverly notched at intervals, in readiness for shorter connector crossbeams to be slotted in, thereby holding the two walls in place. How the workforce executed this part of the operation is a study in teamwork and brawny agility.

The team leaders bellowed out the next set of instructions: 'On to the connector beams!'

Without prompting and certainly without the aid of scaffolding or safety harnesses, four of the stronger men, using only their hands and feet, scaled up the thicker inner pillars to take up positions on the first and the second tiers of the crossbeams, sitting and waiting on the narrow wooden crossbeams. Someone shouted out the correctly numbered connector beam, for all the Lego pieces were pre-numbered. Another hurried to hunt it down before hoisting it up to those waiting on top. One of the acrobats on the first tier grabbed the proffered end and neatly lifted the other end to his counterpart sitting on the opposite crossbeam so that they were both holding the wooden connector. They each placed the cut ends on both sides on the corresponding notches of the original crossbeam. Pausing for a moment, the two men waited for tools to be passed up to them in order to knock the ends into the notches.

With similar economic use of the ropes, the men passed around the only set of tools from one job to another. A large hammerhead was passed to one of the waiting men, an axe doubling up as a hammer at its blunt end was handed up to the other. Wielding their respective tools and still precariously balanced on wooden slats, each strongman one-handedly swung his heavy utensil once, twice, and more when necessary, to hit the connector beam into the notch. This completed, the agile pair high-wired on the ledge to knock the second connector beam in position. The same passing of the tools, the same manual operation, put the second Lego piece in place. They continued to hit the next few connectors down until all of them were in position.

The manoeuvre on the first tier executed, the same process was repeated by another pair perched higher on the second tier of the crossbeam, again sharing the same set of tools. With both tiers of connector beams snugly fitted within the notches, the two wall frameworks were finally secured to each other.

When it was time to lift the third and tallest wall framework, the team pulled and pushed, again and again, but the heavy piece refused to budge. An emergency was taking place and a swift response was called for.

'Where are the women?' Zhaxi shouted. 'Come over quickly, we need your help. Forget the cooking, just come over now!'

Gumi and five other women helpers tending to the firepot ran to the site and quickly positioned themselves on the pull side.

'Der, Nye, Suo!' the shout came louder. It got repeated. And repeated. This time, everyone joined in the shouting. The loud chorus gave a lift to the work team. Slowly the hefty piece moved inch by inch in time to the count. Heave and heave again they continued until the framework was eventually raised and hoisted. The final heft pulled it up directly over the stone platform. Everyone cheered as it stood upright.

This third framework contained a pair of colossal logs to function as the twin pillars in every grandmother's room of a Mosuo house. (For a description of the function of this room see p. 55.) The logs were cut from the same pine trunk, the bigger, lower half serving as the female pillar on the right side of the main room, and the smaller, top half as the male pillar on the left. More symbolisms of the hierarchy of the genders even in the building of a Mosuo house.

On and on the troopers for the day slaved through the morning until the entire framework of the house was all notched up, without one single nail being used. The whole Lego set was finally complete. An incredible sight stood before me. Like a phoenix rising from the ashes, a wooden skeleton of a two-storey structure took shape.

'Time to bless the building of a new home!' Zhaxi bellowed out to an elder waiting for his cue.

Holding a basket filled with highland barley, wheat, buckwheat, rice and corn, the five grains considered indispensable in the Mosuo diet, with sugar and coins thrown in, the elder stepped into the centre of the structure. He faced east, intoned the name of the God of the East, and spoke aloud.

'Bless this new home. Let peace and good fortune follow its occupants,' he chanted, all the while tossing the precious contents of the basket to the heavens. Turning west, he repeated the call, this time beseeching the God of the West. He followed with the same pleas to the Gods of the South and of the North.

Not forgetting all those involved in the building work, Zhaxi arranged a cauldron of stew made from an entire pig to feed and thank them for a hard day's work.

From that day on, things moved swiftly with the construction. On my follow-up visit three months later, the house began to take shape. Most impressive of all was the grandmother's room, built in this case on the second storey of the cottage because of the small land area on which the house sat. This is unconventional from a local perspective, as this room is always on the ground floor, it being the main room of the house. This room is the heart of a Mosuo home, and, following the vernacular, mine was designed to house a stone hearth in the centre. Erected next to the female pillar in this large room was a built-in platform bed fashioned exactly like a typical grandmother's bed. In the opposite corner, the builders mounted a decorative shrine, ready to function as the Tibetan Buddhist place of worship. I was happy to see a perfect replica of a Mosuo grandmother's room.

My bedroom turned out to be a super luxurious 'flower chamber', more suitable for a Mosuo young woman who gets her own room on coming of age. Mine happened to be hotel-suite sized, unlike the smaller functional Mosuo chambers equipped simply with a bed and a small table for the woman to serve tea to her guest. My bed itself was custom-built into the wall and resembled a palatial wedding bed copied from an empress's bedroom. Exquisitely carved wooden casing framed the platform bed. The room was big enough to house a full sofa set. All in all, my boudoir was a little too opulent compared with the humbler indigenous version, but I did not complain.

In designing the house, Zhaxi used hand-carved intricate woodwork for the windows, doorframes, even the cornices. For a finishing touch, every square centimetre on the carved woodwork installed inside and outside the entire house was brilliantly painted in red, blue, green, yellow, pink, purple and every shade in between. Even the ceiling of the grandmother's room was not spared. Looking up, my eyes were treated to a canvas completely filled with mountains, lakes, flowers, longevity symbols and dragons flying in the clouds, all painstakingly hand-painted in a nod to the Sistine Chapel.

As if all this was not enough, the house had a perfect vista over the Moon Lake and an unobstructed view of the sacred Gemu Mountain. Fitted with long sliding windows, each room gave me a bird's eye view of the glorious countryside.

A few Mosuo essentials were not replicated in my house. Every Mosuo home has a special prayer room dedicated to a Tibetan Buddhist shrine housed strategically on higher ground. This room is reserved for the male family member chosen to be a lama, where he can chant, pray and light candles in his home sanctuary.

My house is also missing a typical internal courtyard. If I had the luxury of more acreage, a square courtyard would have been built in the middle of the structure surrounded by rooms all facing inwards. A Mosuo home has more rooms than the usual Chinese farmer's home-stead. There are as many rooms as there are women in the house, plus a common room for the menfolk and a couple more utility rooms. Also missing in my cottage are the barns to house domesticated animals and store produce.

Only part of my house is built of pine logs, the rest of modern materials such as brick, mortar and ordinary wood. Back in the days when the pine forests around Lugu Lake were plentiful, the structure would have been built entirely with interlocking pine logs, made to last hundreds of years. With the present environment-driven moratorium against logging, a modern house in these parts would, like mine, have to make do with commercially available building materials.

Still, my Mosuo home was adequate for my purposes as a second home. Nine months from the day I agreed to build the house and just in time for the Chinese Lunar New Year, Zhaxi handed me the keys to the house.

'Here you are,' he said without much ceremony. 'You can move in.'

I was left almost speechless. All I could say was, 'Thank you very much.'

His effort had far surpassed all my expectations. It was my good fortune that he was the right person for the job. Zhaxi turned out to be the ultimate one-man dream team of designer, architect, builder, project manager, main contractor and fixer. The wonder of it all was that he executed the entire building process without needing any input or supervision from me.

'I will arrange for your new house to be blessed,' Zhaxi told me next, reminding me that owning a traditional Mosuo home smack bang in beautiful Mosuo country is incomplete without the traditional blessing.

'We Mosuos hold a "Bless the Fire Ceremony" before we move into a new house,' he said, adding, 'During the ceremony, we light the first fire on the hearth and invite the Fire God to enter the home.'

Inspired by the idea, I got a Tibetan Buddhist lama friend to divine an auspicious day in January of that year, 2010, for me to move in. At the crack of dawn on that favourable day, the lama friend and his fellow priest clad in their traditional maroon robes turned up at my front door. Sleepy-eyed, I showed them in.

Without further ado, they set up a makeshift altar on the ground in the front yard. On it they placed various religious paraphernalia. Zhaxi and Gizi, the *axia* of his sister Gumi, acting as their assistants, lit up incense and pine branches before the altar, signalling the inauguration of the ceremony.

Sitting cross-legged in the Buddhist tradition, the two lamas began chanting in a low murmur as their eyes followed a sacred text inscribed in a scripture book held by bamboo binding. Sometimes going solo and at other times in unison, the two monks continued their recitation, now and then turning the hallowed pages of their holy book. In pauses between each set of chants, one of them brandished a brush to sprinkle holy water on the altar. At other breaks between prayers, the two assistants took turns to sound a long paean call on a conch shell typically used in Buddhist rituals and beat a constant rhythm on a ceremonial drum.

After a solemn hour and a half, the coterie got ready with a small urn of burning coal and proceeded reverentially up the stairs to my grandmother's room. Quietly I followed behind and stood by to watch as the still-chanting lamas ceremoniously placed the coal fire in the middle of the hearth. More chanting followed as the lamas invited the Fire God to enter the heart of my home.

'The first fire has found its home. The house is blessed,' Zhaxi explained to me quietly.

As the fire took hold, I was reminded to keep it burning throughout my days and never let the embers go out, lest it displeased the fire deity. This would be a challenge, I thought, as lighting a fire was not in my city-bred repertoire. Nevertheless the fire was intended to warm my days and nights and symbolically cook my many meals to come.

With a flourish the lamas sprinkled rice grains around the hearth to ensure I would never go hungry.

For the final touch, the more senior of the lama duo presented me with a *thangka* scroll depicting the Buddha of Fortune. Zhaxi, acting his part as assistant, took the *thangka* and hung it up ceremoniously by the Buddhist altar in the corner. After kowtowing three times to it, he motioned me to do the same. Dutifully I followed suit.

On the morning after, I woke up to the sound of the resident cockerel crowing. I began the first day in my newly blessed home with what would become my daily morning ritual. With a cup of freshly brewed Yunnan Arabica coffee in hand, I ventured out to the sun-drenched terrace running alongside the whole house and waited for the theatre of the countryside to unfold before me.

From a vantage point perched on a small hillock, I took in the view before me. A small circle of pine-forested hills ringed the tranquil Moon Lake, so called because of its crescent shape. To its left the grand old Gemu Mountain seemed to be smiling down on me.

I took ten slow, deep breaths, filling my lungs with the crisp, clear air. I could not get cleaner air than this, I mused to myself, for this remote mountainous corner of Yunnan, along with Tibet and Hainan, are the only three provinces that are off the pollution map of China – a nice change from the congested air I breathe in Chinese cities.

All was quiet by the lakefront. There was no sign of life from my nearest and only neighbour by the lake. In the hushed silence as in a theatre just before the curtain goes up, I took the first sip of my morning coffee, sensing that the performance was about to begin.

Against the backdrop of a cloudless sky of the bluest blue, I spied a pair of eagles circling the lake with a determined but measured effort. Slowly, now flying high and making big circles, now swooping down low and close to the lake surface, the pair eyed the wild ducks which had taken winter refuge here from the cold Siberian north. Quick as lightning, one of the eagles suddenly swept down on a duckling wading near the lakeshore. A panicked rush ensued, punctuated by loud quacking sounding the imminent danger. A whole flock of ducks took to the sky in flight and fright, just in time for the intended victim to escape the vicious claws of the eagle, which now retreated to join its partner for another go. The curtain came down on Act One.

On a perfect morning, there was no better show than this. I took another sip of my coffee just as hundreds of noisy ducks returned. They figured it was now safe to settle down to feed and frolic on Moon Lake once again.

And so the theatre of the Lugu Lake countryside continued. I caught the subsequent acts from the grandmother's room upstairs. As I entered, I went up to the Buddhist altar to light some jasmine incense sticks. I turned to my Tibetan prayer bowls. On this first morning, I chose the largest one shaped like a round fish bowl but made of burnished, beaten bronze. Taking the sounding rod, I tapped its side and rolled the rod smoothly but firmly round its rim, once, twice, thrice. The first hum began softly and then crescendoed slowly to a louder bass as I offered the sonorous hymn to the morning.

Looking out of the wide window, I gazed at the holy female mountain and saw clouds hovering round her nearly 4,000-metre peak. It reminded me of the folktale according to which Gemu is always a reliable weather vane. 'Gemu wearing a cloud hat means rain will come,' one of my friends once told me.

Although Gemu looks her best from the south side, my side of this sacred mountain on the north has a different face to it, much like a lion in repose. Hence her other sobriquet – the Lion Mountain. Luckily for me this is by far the quieter and less touristy side.

Crossing over to the other side will take me to the front face of the mountain whose silhouette is unmistakably that of the imposing reclining figure of the Goddess as she guards over Lugu Lake. It is there by the side of the big lake that the tourists gather. Indeed the villages around the big lake have grown to be burgeoning tourist destinations over the last decade.

Buses make a beeline to disembark tourists at the cable car station on that side of the mountain to take in an aerial view on their way to Gemu's cave at the top of the mountain. In a funny twist to what must have been a direct translation from a Chinese–English dictionary, the signpost in front of the cable car station reads in English: 'Goddess Hole Ropeway'.

The cave advertises itself as the 'home' of Gemu Goddess, complete with a boudoir cave romantically billed as her flower chamber where she entertains her lovers. Next to her private bedroom, stalagmites are grouped together shaped suspiciously like proud phalluses, symbols of virility and worship to the locals. The Mosuo community in the small hamlets and villages facing that side of Lugu Lake, including picturesque Lige, has welcomed the march of tourism into its midst with open arms. Almost every family there is involved one way or another in the tourist business.

But my side of the Goddess Mountain is shielded from the madness of the tourist pack. My cottage sits in the middle between the busy touristy Lugu Lake side and the vast farmland sitting on the plains below Gemu. The traffic passing in front of my house, if any, is typically a small group of farmers walking their way home from collecting firewood in the surrounding hills or the occasional lone motorcyclist passing by. Otherwise the noiselessness offers me a quietness so still I can almost hear it.

As I count myself lucky to be living in such a perfect corner of north-east Yunnan, I still marvel at the extraordinary turn of events – from a chance remark by Zhaxi to my living in a charming cottage built on this little piece of heaven on earth. My home may be humble by the standards of holiday villas in southern Europe but it is by far the most eye-catching and well-appointed mansion in these parts.

In the beginning I treated my dwelling-place as a holiday home, retreating there every couple of months for rest and recreation when I tired of the hectic city life of Singapore, Beijing or London. I got used to living in the country, adjusting to draughty wintry nights, frozen water pipes in the morning and intermittent power outages during peak tourist seasons.

Still umbilically tied to modern conveniences, I gradually sent over boxes filled with things I could not do without – a coffee-bean grinder and its accompanying coffee maker, a trusty goose-down duvet, battery-charged camping lights, tough-wearing sporting jackets, sturdy hiking boots, a hair dryer and the many bottles of cosmetics and toiletries unavailable in the wilds of Yunnan. I filled my Apple phone with endless tracks of music to play on quiet nights while I rifled through two shelves full of history and travel books and novels I had sent over.

I could at last settle in to what would become the spiritual home for my feminist soul.

3

Going Native

Acquiring a new second home nudged me into a honeymoon state of mind. I was itching to spend time in my Mosuo house. I was excited each time I planned a return visit, bringing things that would slowly transform the house into a home. Over time I found myself spending more and more time in Lugu Lake than in my house in Singapore. I took time to make new friends, and without setting out to live like a local I found myself inching closer to becoming an old hand in the ways of the Mosuos.

'She is one of us,' a close Mosuo friend of mine declared recently after knowing me for the past six years. 'She is already half Mosuo!'

I felt vindicated. It was nice to know that my approach of not acting or appearing to be too different from the locals had paid off. I was after all a foreigner trying to fit in with a traditionally closed-off community still steeped in many of their old ways and customs.

Careful not to step on any toes or cause any misunderstanding, I intuitively put myself to the test each time I walked out the door, not knowing where things would lead me.

One of my first encounters with doing things the native way had to do with a bare necessity, that of answering nature's call. Arriving at my goddaughter's home for the first time and after spending the afternoon bonding with my new 'family', I quite naturally needed to go.

'Where is the toilet?' I asked.

'Our home has no toilet,' Ladzu replied innocently.

This turned out to be the norm. A lavatory in a Mosuo home is still a luxury. Surprisingly a lot of these homes have not caught up with the rest of rural China. For instance, in my grandfather's village deep inside Guangdong province, every farmhouse would at least have a bathroom with a shower and a squatting toilet.

I panicked. It must have shown on my face.

'Why don't I show you outside?' she added, reading my expression.

Leading me to a side door, Ladzu pushed it open and stood aside for me to pass through.

'There?' I asked, glancing around the backyard.

She nodded and left me to my own devices.

I was at a loss as to how to proceed. Before me was a bare patch of ground next to the potato plot. Grazing about were a horse and a couple of chickens. A mud-and-straw wall separated the yard from the neighbours.

'Where in this wide open space does one do it?' I asked myself.

Several logistical problems came to mind. Where was the most inconspicuous place to do what I must do? Which was the most strategic spot to remain unseen by the neighbours? Which plant or animal life would I be poisoning? How far away from the irrigation drain should I position myself so as not to pollute the water?

After hesitating for a while, I decided on the farthest corner of the yard, away from the house. Bracing myself, I squatted down and finally did the deed.

The problem with this sort of thing was that it would have to be repeated on my subsequent visits. With each repeat performance, new questions arose. Should I pick the same or a new spot? Would it be better to leave behind a paper trail or spread it around? Should I, like a dog, kick some mud to hide the evidence? Where was the spade when I most needed it?

Eventually I got used to the idea as I made many more visits to this humble home without a lavatory. In the early days of my sojourn before my house was built, Gumi had always insisted that I stayed over after a late dinner. Their courtyard home is large and there were always a couple of empty rooms to bunk in. I accepted her hospitality gladly, knowing full well that I would have to venture out in the night for my nocturnal pit stops.

A night-time ritual always turned out to be a nightmare. Gumi's place was situated at the edge of a tiny farming hamlet whose homes had only been connected with electricity a few years before. Street lighting had yet to be installed along the tracks running through the hamlet. Being used to complete pitch-darkness, the villagers have no problem seeing where they are going in the night. Heavily bespectacled, I have poor night vision even in the best of well-lit times. My nocturnal visits to the unlit backyard were traumatic episodes, with me having to balance a torch in one hand while doing my thing in the inky blackness of the night.

After a while I learnt to go with the flow and say nonchalantly, 'I am going outside', to mean you-know-what. I did not dwell on the matter any more until I ventured out to my favourite spot in the same backyard on a return visit months later. Seeing the same patch of ground in a new light, I realized to my horror that the by-now not inconsequential paper trail I had left behind on my earlier visits was such an offensive eyesore. I was appalled to realize that I was the guilty party.

'Aren't these bits of tissue paper supposed to be biodegradable, for heaven's sake?' I said to myself. 'Doesn't anybody else use paper?'

Quietly ashamed, I knew I had to clean up. I retreated to fetch a plastic bag and a pair of tongs, and like a thief in the night surreptitiously picked up my own paper debris, dumping the lot in the nearest garbage heap.

Adopting a name easily pronounceable to the locals is, I suppose, also part of going native. When I first came to Lugu Lake, I took it upon myself to be called 'Ah Hong', the way my family calls me at home. 'Hong' is the last of my two-part given name, WaiHong, a name chosen by my paternal grandfather who had the right and obligation to name all his grandchildren, following the traditional Chinese custom. The first of my two-part name, 'Wai', denotes that I am a girl and that I belong to the third generation of grandfather Choo. The given names of all my female cousins are 'Wai-something', the 'something' being the defining individual name of each one of us in that generation. Mine was 'Hong', and the use of 'Ah' prefixing this part of my given name denotes familiarity. I wanted the locals to be as informal with me as my own family.

Being 'Ah Hong' worked out pretty well until one day someone referred to me as 'Majang Ah Hong', meaning the Ah Hong who lived on the horse farm, 'Majang' in Chinese. This made sense, as I lived in a house built on a horse farm. The nickname stuck. I even liked the sound and feel of it. My four-syllabic nickname happened to sound like the double dual-syllable form of a Mosuo name. Like Cher'er Lazuo or Zhaxi Pinzuo. So the four sounds of my nickname fitted.

The double name of a Mosuo is given to her on the day she is born, not by her grandfather, like the Chinese, but by a religious leader. Traditionally, a *daba*, a village shaman, would choose a name for the infant in an intricate naming ceremony. There are not too many old Mosuo names to come by and certainly no name is gender specific to a girl or boy. I have many Mosuo friends of either gender having the same names.

Since Tibetan Buddhism made its way to Lugu Lake 400 or so years ago, the job of naming a person has been taken over by Buddhist lamas. Running short of Mosuo names, the priests have resorted to borrowing Tibetan names, so much so that the names of many Mosuos I have met, such as Zhaxi the builder, are Tibetan.

Happy as I of the horse farm was with my nickname, it never occurred to me to get myself a Mosuo name until one New Year's Day when I went to pay my respects to a friend who is a Buddhist lama. We were chatting after a festive meal when Duojie lama mentioned that the Mosuo Living Buddha, Luosang Yishi, happened to be in residence in Yongning. A Tibetan Buddhist lama who has reached the rank of a Living Buddha ranks just below the highest offices of the Dalai Lama and the Panchen Lama in the hierarchy of the faith. There are across the country several hundreds of Living Buddhas but very few of them are Mosuos.

'The Living Buddha coming back for the New Year is a rare occasion. Would you like to request a name from him?' Duojie asked out of the blue.

'Er, you mean now?' I said meekly.

'Yes, if we can catch him today. I can drive you over now and make a request for a name to be given to you.'

Off we went. I was literally being carried along with the idea, but as I mulled it over while riding in the car I realized that it would be a momentous event in my life if I were to become Mosuo.

Arriving at the imposing residence of the Living Buddha situated by the oldest Tibetan Buddhist monastery of Zhamei Si in Yongning, Duojie and I were ushered into a hall and told to wait for an audience. Duojie explained my request to an assistant.

'His Holiness is unwell today,' his secretary told us. 'He will probably not be able to see you in person, but we have passed him your request. Please wait. I am sure he will grant you a name.'

There were a few other villagers with us in the hall. We all waited for what seemed like an interminable spell. I think I might even have dozed off for a while. The tea served to us was cold by the time the secretary rushed back into the waiting hall.

'Here it is!' he said, waving a piece of paper in his hand. 'The Living Buddha took some moments to decide on the most appropriate name for you and this is the one he has chosen.'

The words 'Ercher Dzuoma', was written in bold Tibetan writing on the paper he handed to us.

So this was my new Mosuo name, exactly the same as that of two of my local female friends. The first part of the name, Ercher, means 'precious', and the second, Dzuoma, a manifestation of the Green Buddha. This form of the Buddha carries with it a capacity to be compassionate and of a giving nature. The Mosuos believe that a given name endows its recipient with the qualities suggested by its meaning. My two friends and I have a lot to live up to.

Being given a new local name has yet to give me new insight or inspiration, I must admit. However, it did give me a fresh sense of belonging in a small way whenever I introduced myself as Ercher Dzuoma to a Mosuo person. The common reaction was a warm smile, often followed with the words 'That is a nice name.'

Having a local name was one thing, but I needed to dress the part. Gumi insisted I did just that when her family and I were about to set off for the village party on New Year's Eve.

'You must dress in the Mosuo way for this occasion,' she said. 'You can wear an outfit of mine. I will help you to put it on.'

Rummaging through a pile of clothes, Gumi pulled out a long, white, pleated skirt and a few other pieces of clothing. I recognized them from the coming-of-age ceremony. As Gumi dressed me up, we encountered a slight problem – my not so discreet waist, as Gumi discovered when she struggled to cinch the broad pink cummerbund round it. We managed in the end. She finished me off by squeezing on my head a braided bejewelled headdress weighing a ton.

All togged up and feeling like a colourful stuffed cucumber, I trailed behind Gumi and her two children, who would become my godchildren, clumsily holding the too-long skirt as we made our way through the muddy path to the village basketball court where the New Year party was in full swing. I looked around and was devastated to find that I was the only adult female wearing the native costume. Gumi and the other women wore their everyday blouse-and-pants outfits. Only the teenage girls and their younger siblings were in full gear.

My only consolation for dressing up was being rewarded by the village head, who passed round a red packet of good-luck money to each of the kids and me for our sartorial efforts. To top it all, the handsomest bloke at the party led me by the hand to lead in the dance circle.

My wardrobe now consists of three different traditional outfits and two headdresses, which I alternate for different formal occasions, whether it is a coming-of-age ceremony, a house-blessing party or the Mountain Goddess Festival.

Looking the part of one who has gone native was easy compared to walking the walk like a Mosuo. Getting about like the locals was the next challenge facing me. Before the invention of the wheel and definitely before the advent of the locomotive engine, the locals went about on foot or horseback. Everyone walked miles everywhere. On a daily basis, my godson took 45 minutes on foot to get to school. Farmers walked with basketfuls of produce on their backs on their daily treks to the market two to three hours away. For a longer journey, and to them this meant at least more than half a day's walk, villagers jumped on their horses and rode off to their destinations.

In the beginning, I walked everywhere. Shod in hiking boots, I would set out on foot from my tourist digs in Lige towards the hamlet of Baju where my two godchildren lived.

'It is not far away,' the kids told me. 'We will meet you halfway.'

That halfway point, somewhere beyond hillocks and dales along narrow, winding paths past grazing cows, seemed a long way off as I exerted myself in the thin air at an altitude of nearly 3,000 metres above sea level. Ladzu and Nongbu waiting on a hilltop ahead was a most welcomed sight.

Having conquered the art of walking, I decided it was time to move up a notch and learn to ride a horse. Everyone here rode, from the youngest child to the oldest adult. I had never ridden in my whole life and, if truth be told, I had always been a little frightened of going near an animal as big as a horse.

Actually the opportunity to ride a horse came about not so much by choice as by a last resort in desperate times. I had recklessly joined a small hiking group on an eight-day hike-and-camp trip on the ancient tea-horse trail from Lugu Lake in Yunnan to the Yadin National Park in the neighbouring province of Sichuan. The long hike entailed criss-crossing the mountain ridges at the eastern end of the Himalayan range. En route we would scale picturesque highlands, trek alongside roaring white waters, sight whole herds of yak cattle in their natural high-plateau habitat, smell my first azalea on a verdant meadow, pick fragrant white snow tea on a high peak and stand in awe of the mighty three-peaked, snow-capped Kongka mountain range sacred to the Tibetans.

It was a chance to walk on a part of the old tea-horse trail hewn out of the vast mountainous region to allow traders in the past millennium to carry tea grown in China over the edge of the Himalayas to Tibet and beyond. On their return, the traders of old would bring back Tibetan horses to sell on to the imperial army. Those enterprising and hardy merchants of long ago would set out on their long journeys in large horse packs, walking alongside their heavily laden horses and mules.

Our enthusiastic bunch of three city girls had our own horse pack of three horses and two mules led by two stable hands. A mountain guide plotted our way as we hiked at a fast clip of 25 kilometres a day, going uphill most of the time. We reached a plateau as high as 4,500 metres on the fourth day.

At this stage I began to feel the worst effects of altitude sickness. My face and hands were swollen, my head hurt constantly and I felt a deep fatigue overcoming me.

'I give up,' I said to the guide. 'I cannot walk one more step. Please take me back to base camp.'

'No,' said the guide who would have none of it.

Without saying another word, he unloaded our camping gear off a squat workhorse, tied a small wooden saddle on to its back and heaved me up on to it. That was my maiden ride on horseback.

This was no ride for a beginner. As I gingerly took hold of the reins and got used to the rhythm of my mount, the first of the summer rains poured down on us. We stopped to put on our raingear. By the time we set off again, the mountain trail had turned into a swampy mud path. Under my weight the poor horse squished and squashed his way forward on the narrow trail. But unlike its wobbly rider, the animal trudged on steadily.

Up and on we continued for the next few days. I reached the highest point of our trip at 5,000 metres on horseback, relieved that I had mastered the art of leaning forward when going uphill and backward downhill. By the time we arrived at the magnificent nature reserve of Yadin, I knew I could ride like a native.

Back home in Lugu Lake, I showed off my new riding skills by arriving on horseback at the Gemu Goddess Festival that summer. In full traditional gear, I rode in on a handsome mount draped with a red and gold dragon blanket with bindings to match, ringing its horse-bell around its neck as we cut through the crowd.

The horse and its rider made a festive pair. As we made our way on to the fairground, locals who recognized me nodded and smiled. On seeing a picture opportunity, an eager tourist rushed forward to train his camera on us, clicking away and shouting to his friends.

'Quick! Here's a Mosuo!'

As the rest of China has galloped into the twenty-first century, driving its Ferraris along the highways leading to Beijing and riding electric motorcycles in the lanes of Kunming, the Mosuo heartland has not been slow in catching up with the city folk.

Owning a motorbike was a dream come true for every macho Mosuo man. His more affluent cousin would drive around in a small family car while the really affluent, at least in local terms, would zoom about on the few tarmac roads in a land cruiser or SUV.

For some time I had wondered whether or not to get a car. I missed driving and longed to be more mobile. After mentioning this in passing to Zhaxi, the builder of my home, he could not mask his excitement and immediately appointed himself to be my buying agent.

'You should buy a big-model four-wheel drive for sure,' he suggested. 'That way, you can drive around the mountain roads. You must make sure the car has a high enough floorboard. We have too many fallen rocks on the road here,' he added.

When it came time to go on a buying trip to the nearest city of Lijiang, Zhaxi appeared with an entourage comprising his friend the local car mechanic and a number of his male friends and relatives. Our group of eight made its way to a car showroom. All eyes lit up when we were shown a row of SUVs for sale.

The men coalesced into a buying committee, examining the engines and checking out the height of the floorboards of each model. Like kids in a candy store, they were enjoying the vicarious pleasure of buying a man-sized vehicle.

'This one is the best model,' the car mechanic gave his verdict after huddling with the rest of the committee. I liked the white Mitsubishi Leopard he pointed out.

'No, not white. It must be army green,' Zhaxi chipped in as the rest nodded in approval.

'Why green?' I asked, feeling I was losing what little say I had in the matter.

'Because it is the colour local officials and the big bosses like the most. If you drive a green car like this, no traffic police will stop you. And everyone else on the road will give way to you, thinking you are a VIP!'

That was that. The committee had voted. All that was left was for me to pay up and drive the new green monster away.

A few days later I drove to Baju village to meet some friends. Duojie, my lama friend, saw me in the car.

'Have you had the car blessed?' he asked.

'A car needs to be blessed?' I replied.

'Yes, just to be on the safe side.'

Duojie offered to do the honours there and then. Parking the car in front of his house, I stood aside as he brought out the tools of his trade. He started chanting. Then he sprinkled holy water on the outside of the car. Opening the car door on the driver side, he took some rice grains from a brass prayer bowl and tossed them about in the interior of the car as he continued chanting.

'I will have to clean that out later,' I thought to myself.

At the end of the car-blessing ceremony, Duojie produced a long yellow scarf.

'This *hadaq* is special. It was blessed in the Potala Palace in Lhasa,' he said, tying it ceremoniously into a knotted sash and hanging it on the rear-view mirror above the driver's seat.

'This will keep you safe from any traffic accident,' he concluded.

Driving around the Mosuo countryside has its own unique etiquette rules. In a community that values the 'Help thy Neighbour' commandment, a car owner is expected to offer rides to friends walking by.

Riding as a passenger in Gizi's farm truck one day, we passed a group of five women walking with laden shopping baskets on their backs. Gizi stopped to give them a lift to town. They piled happily on to the open truck at the back. A few minutes later, an elderly woman and her granddaughter who were standing by the roadside hailed him down. They too joined the others on the truck. Before long we had a truckload of ten villagers at the back of the lorry.

I took the lesson to heart. I have since made it a habit to give passers-by a ride whenever possible. Once, a woman with a teenage girl waved me down frantically. I stopped, only to discover in shock that the girl's foot was bleeding profusely.

'Get in quickly!' I said to the mother as I opened the passenger door. They got in.

'To the hospital?' I asked.

The mother nodded, all the while holding the wound tightly.

I broke the speed limit to reach the hospital within ten minutes.

Offering rides to friends sometimes came with unimagined consequences. A young goatherd friend of mine asked me to give him a lift to a wedding. I had not expected to see him coming towards my car with a live goat in tow.

'This is my wedding gift to the couple,' he said.

Never in my life had I ever seen such a lively wedding present. He bagged the goat and loaded it up in the trunk of my car. The gift bleated all the way. Finally it was unloaded on arrival. The goatherd nonchalantly carried the parcel out, took the goat out of the bag and proudly walked in with his present.

Having walked the walk of the Mosuos, I had yet to talk their talk. This turned out to be the most challenging task I had set myself. The Mosuo language has no written script. Theirs is an entirely oral language passed on from one generation to the next by word of mouth. They put nothing down on paper. Except for the younger generations who have had the opportunity to attend school for the last 20 years or so, older Mosuos are illiterate in the true sense of the word.

The locals love to recount the story of how they lost the written word. The Na people had a written language a long time ago. The learned *dabas* read and wrote in the Mosuo language. The language took the form of hieroglyphs, whose traces can be seen on old divination sticks still used by *dabas* for their religious ceremonies today. No one, however, knows how to decipher these ancient symbols any longer.

In the story, two *dabas* were on their way to a faraway village to conduct an important ritual. As was the custom, they carried their scripture with them. The religious verses, written in the old language, were etched on leather sheets.

Owing to inclement weather, their journey took much longer than planned and they ran out of food. Hungry and tired, they stopped to rest. Much as they tried, they could not find any edible plants in the remote mountains. Desperate, they turned to each other with the same thought.

'Why don't we boil the leather sheets and eat them?'

And that was the last of Mosuo writing, lost in the digestive tracts of the holy duo.

Learning an oral language is baffling to someone used to the written word. Throughout my life I have learnt languages the classical way. I read and write the words on paper at the same time as I hear them spoken before repeating the sounds orally. That was the way I learnt Mandarin from kindergarten through primary school, and that was the way I started my English schooling at the age of 11. All four elements, reading, writing, hearing and speaking, work together in tandem. Take away the reading and writing bits and I will be at a loss, as I have found out in the aural-oral realm of the Mosuo language.

It is not for want of trying that I have yet to master this language. I make my friends repeat Mosuo words again and again. The sounds are alien to me, bearing no resemblance whatsoever to Chinese or English, or even to the French, Italian or Spanish of which I have a passing knowledge. They sound strangely Russian to my untutored ear, with consonants sounding like 'dz', 'khr', 'zhy' and 'nya'. Even the inflection of the words in a sentence follows a strain I have never heard before. To make matters worse, a Mosuo sentence is constructed in reverse to the language systems I know, with the subject and object coming out front before ending with the verb.

I have tried devising my own alphabet system to imitate the Mosuo sounds but with little success. When I repeat what I have written down in my rough-cut system, the words come out all wrong and are incomprehensible to my friends. I have even tried using some other alphabet system I read in a scholarly work but found it equally unfathomable. Try as I might, nothing seems to work.

For now I make do with saying the basics in Mosuo, resorting to Mandarin when I want to carry a conversation further.

Going some way to becoming a native was made possible when my early short-term stays grew longer and more frequent. I ended up with making at least three to four visits a year, staying in my Mosuo home for a couple of months at each stretch. I grew accustomed to shuttling between Singapore and Lugu Lake, navigating between a hectic city life and a different rural rhythm in the mountains.

It is like leading two separate lives. With one foot in my home in Singapore, I have chosen to plant the other foot in a place and an environment entirely different.

In my original skin, I look back with nostalgia on a frenzied previous life as a lawyer in Singapore. I took and continue to take breaks to visit family in Amsterdam and San Francisco and friends in Beijing and London, which I enjoy tremendously.

For my other life, I live in an undeveloped corner of China where the people still carry on living and farming the way their foremothers and forefathers did hundreds of years ago. I like the escape to this separate life in Lugu Lake. In the six years since, I have proven to myself that I can rough it out in making a life among the Mosuos.

While there I hang around with Mosuo friends. I sense that they treat me not so much as an outsider in their midst but as an insider. I am included in the local guest list when my closer friends celebrate their major life events. Often I am the only foreigner present at family meals. My presence is expected at village activities, coming-of-age ceremonies and funerals. A few confide their secrets to me. I am gratified that I have in some way become a part of their lives.

In many ways I really believe I am accepted because I am a woman welcomed into a woman's world. In this female-dominated bubble, no one thinks it strange that I am a lone female who goes about happily on my own. The Mosuos, both women and men, are accustomed to the presence of a strong woman mainly because every home has one.

Furthermore I think my Mosuo friends are aware of how comfortable I feel moving around in a community that celebrates the female. There is, I am sure, a mutual understanding that we are of one mind.

This in itself is a revelation, the full impact of which I have yet to digest. It is strange but true that in my entire life I have never felt so at ease in an environment that accepts me for what I am. I feel cocooned within a cosmos that allows and encourages me as a woman to be me without asking for more. Not to belabour the point, not once have I felt ignored in voicing an opinion or suggesting a course of action. At no time have I felt the need to fight against a tide of ignorance or open animosity towards woman-friendly issues. Never have I felt pushed to demand or fight for a wrong committed against me because I am a woman. Intuitively I feel very much at home with the Mosuos.

To this day I am still amazed how it took a village to deconstruct the corporate lawyer in me, and a matriarchal tribe to build up the feminist consciousness in my native heart.

4

Getting to Know
the Mosuos

Just as I was starting to explore the world of the Mosuos as an outsider looking in, a serendipitous turn came along my way when a teenage girl befriended me at the Gemu Mountain Goddess Festival and opened a door to her family and eventually an entire community.

Ladzu, the 14-year-old girl with a winning smile at the festival, was the first Mosuo I met. Exchanging pleasantries, I told her I wanted to learn the Mosuo language.

'Would you teach me?' I asked.

'Of course!' she said.

'Shall I call you "teacher" then?'

'No, no! You mustn't,' Ladzu protested. 'You are my elder and cannot possibly address me in such a respectful manner. Why not let me call you godmother?'

'Sure,' I responded, without giving it a second thought, not realizing how far that spur-of-the-moment connection would lead me. From then on, we became a close maternal pair under the gaze of her amused family. So began my Mosuo adventure, and, as I think back, it was fitting that it took this female bond for me to gain entry into the

Kingdom of Women.

My goddaughter is the firstborn of her Mosuo mother and her long-term *axia*, or common-law husband as we would understand it. He is not a Mosuo himself but a Pumi, coming from a mountain tribe that is linguistically and culturally close to the Mosuos, except that it is not matriarchal. Having met a strong Mosuo woman, he left home to move in with her on her farm and has stayed on ever since.

When Ladzu was born, she was the delight of her mother and her *axia* and the darling of her maternal grandmother for being her first female grandchild. Before Ladzu, two grandsons had been born to the grandmother's family. Consistent with Mosuo custom, the grandmother would have treated the arrival of the first girl in the third generation with the greatest joy, because that would mean her maternal bloodline could carry on.

Contrast this with the reaction of a grandmother in any other community in China and we will find the exact opposite scenario. In olden times, a Chinese grandmother would have treated the arrival of a girl baby as a disaster, especially if the baby followed a string of only daughters born to the family. The reason is in direct contrast to the matrilineal tenet of the Mosuos. Only the birth of a son in a patriarchal Chinese family is a joyous event. Without a male heir to carry on the family name, its paternal bloodline would come to an end. An abandoned baby even in present-day China would more likely be a girl than a boy.

Ladzu has a brother three years younger than her, Nongbu, the same boy whose coming-of-age ceremony I would conduct in due course. When Ladzu anointed me as her godmother, Nongbu insisted that I too recognize him as my godson. The then 11-year-old was bright, mischievous and full of energy, easily winning me over.

My new godchildren, part of a string of other godchildren collected over the years as a divorcee with no children of my own, had enthusiastically invited me over to their home when we parted at the Gemu Festival. They explained that their home was situated in a small hamlet on the far side of the Goddess Mountain. When I arrived the following day with my chauffeur, their mother was surprised to find a stranger at her door.

'Oh dear, the children have forgotten to tell her I was coming,' I thought to myself.

With an embarrassed nod, I said hello and was gladdened that she returned my greeting with an easy smile and warm welcome. Her children introduced me as their 'Ganma', godmother in Chinese.

'Since you are their Ganma, and older than me, I will call you Amur,' she said, explaining that it meant 'older sister' in Mosuo. 'You can call me Gumi. That means younger sister in Mosuo.'

Not missing a beat, Gumi invited me to stay for lunch. I would discover over time that the Mosuos are like that, never hesitating to extend their hospitality to a guest, even an uninvited one.

'What would you like for lunch, chicken or duck?' she asked.

'Chicken would be nice,' I said, not realizing that by those very words I was condemning to an early demise one of the chickens clucking about in the courtyard.

'Right,' said Gumi to her son, 'go catch a chicken, Nongbu.'

Without further ado, little Nongbu ran after a brood of chickens and after some struggle managed to chase one down. Handily, he grabbed both claws and passed lunch over to his mother. Gumi took hold of the chicken, tied up its legs and simply put it aside. She surprised me by ignoring the chicken as she went about her other kitchen chores.

It was only when her *axia* returned home an hour later that she motioned to him with these words:

'The chicken is over there.'

Without missing a beat, he knew exactly what she meant. Arming himself with a meat cleaver, he grabbed the chicken and quickly slaughtered it. He proceeded to de-feather, clean and cut it up before handing the pot-ready chicken to her.

'Why did you wait for him to slaughter the chicken?' I asked Gumi.

'We Mosuo women never do any killing of life,' she said. 'We never touch a dead person or have anything to do with preparing a corpse for cremation.'

A slice of unique Mosuo life unfolded right before my very eyes from the time Nongbu chased down the chicken to it being killed and prepared for cooking over a wood fire in the hearth. It boils down to the special place created for women in Mosuo society. Understanding that the wellspring of new life resides in women, this society believes in the sanctity of women as representing life and light.

Upholding life and light means a distancing away from death, whether it is taking the life of an animal or handling a corpse directly or indirectly. To keep this taboo sacrosanct, a Mosuo woman does not, and must not, kill any animal or other living thing. The men handle the dirty jobs. Likewise, a Mosuo woman does not, and must not, have anything to do with touching or preparing a dead body for its funeral. The men have to perform this unsavoury task.

I was reminded of this beautiful allegory when I saw Gumi waiting for her man to kill the chicken for my lunch. Time and again I would see the same tableau replayed whenever a farm animal was to be slaughtered, with the woman walking away to shield her eyes while the man carried out the killing and cleaning, returning only when he was ready with the butchered meat.

This gallant and protective act makes me envy the Mosuo woman, who must feel special and glad that she is a woman. This is quite the opposite to anything I have experienced in a chauvinistic Chinese household where my grandmother, who did all the cooking for the family, had to perform all manner of kitchen chores big and small, including the killing of live fish, chickens and ducks. The men in the house would have nothing to do with these menial womanly tasks.

Ladzu's home life had more stories to reveal about the special position women hold in Mosuo life. For instance, her home is the home of her mother, not her father.

'This land belongs to me,' Gumi explained. 'My mother gave me part of the land she owned after I told her my *axia* was moving in with me.'

Home to Gumi and her *axia*, whom I was to address as 'Gizi', younger brother, is a simple rectangular courtyard surrounded on four sides of its perimeter by pine-log structures. The main structure is a large all-purpose room known as 'the grandmother's room'. As in all Mosuo homes, Gumi uses the room to serve multiple uses, as the bedroom for the grandmother of the family, as well as housing the heater-cum-stove in the form of the family hearth, the kitchen, the sitting and dining room, and the cooling place to hang salted pork cured from home-raised pigs.

On the other three sides of the courtyard are four bedrooms and three other rooms used for storage of grain and potatoes grown on the family farm. In a nod to modern times, Gumi and Gizi made sure to have the all-important television-cum-family room. A barn outside the courtyard is used to keep a litter of pigs, chickens, ducks and geese, and a water buffalo, the workhorse for the farm. In a good year, Gumi may add a cow or a horse.

Her farm behind the house measures nearly seven *mou* (slightly over one acre), large enough to grow rice for the family and for barter, as well as maize and potatoes to feed both her family and the farm animals. Although Gumi does not carry out any herding, some of her neighbours tend mountain goat and sheep for meat and wool.

The owner-cum-manager of the subsistence farm and home is none other than Gumi, clearly the head of this farmstead. As the boss, she plans everything for the farm, deciding all the planting and harvesting schedules and the kind and number of animals to keep. She is the type of boss who walks the walk, getting her hands dirty in putting her plans into action. Other than enlisting the help of Gizi to lift heavy objects or carry out the more arduous tasks, she carries out most of the burdens of farm work, going out with a sickle to cut wild pig grass in the morning, walking back with a laden basket on her back, shredding it by hand and mixing it with chopped potatoes and rice bran for the pigs' supper, feeding all the other farm animals, planting, harvesting and storing rice, corn and potatoes, cooking all the meals and making sure there is always enough food not only for her family but also for the animals. She is also, unsurprisingly, the money manager. Significantly, Gizi was the one who confirmed the arrangement to me.

'Gumi is in charge of money at home. She keeps the money we get if we sell any crops or farm animals. She keeps all the money I earn outside as a wood-cutter. I get spending money from her. I give in to all her decisions about money.'

A Chinese woman would give anything to be in the position of Gumi in her female-dominated household. In the traditional Chinese countryside, no woman would hold the equivalent of title deeds to any property. Strictly following the family bloodline, property passes solely from grandfather to father to son. Nor would the wife of the house have any power to control the finances of the family. Her husband would call all the shots. While the wife may generally administer the expenses for the household, more often than not her husband would hold the real purse strings and dole out money to the wife.

Modern life in Chinese cities may see some of these male-dominated practices lose their hold, mainly due to women being educated, working and earning money alongside their male counterparts. Even so, the basic tenets remain. I have a good friend who is an entrepreneur in Beijing. Both his parents are university graduates holding down middle-class jobs but his grandparents were farmers in the countryside.

'I am expected as a son to look after my parents in their old age. I meet their bigger expenses. This is not expected of my sister. Anyway, she is married with kids and belongs to her husband's side, so she doesn't count,' he said when I broached the subject of how patriarchy affected him.

Going back to the world Gumi inhabits, how she manages her farm is for me a lesson in community living. Gumi rang me one day when my visit coincided with the time of year for planting crops.

'I will be planting rice tomorrow. Want to come over and watch?'

By the time I got to Gumi's house the following morning, a group of women had gathered in her courtyard and were finishing up their breakfast of steamed buns and tea.

'Let's start,' Gumi said as she wound a long scarf around her head. Bare-footed but clad in long sleeves and work pants, Gumi and her eight friends made their way to the rice field behind the house.

Each of them grabbed a bundle of rice saplings which Gumi had previously sprouted in a corner of the farm and stepped on to the wet rice field. They waded through the inundated field and lined themselves up in a row.

As if on cue, they started to move at the same instant, separating the saplings from the bundle, bending over and planting the rice sapling by sapling in a neat row. Together the nine women worked in time to a silent rhythm, gathering pace as they finished the first row. Deftly they stepped back to start on the next row of saplings.

When they reached the third row, Gumi, who is known in her

village as *the voice*, suddenly broke out in song. Other voices joined in the folksong, cheering each other on. On and on these hardy women continued until the sun stood overhead.

Gumi ran back home to prepare food for the gang. Sodden from head to toe, her work mates trooped back, resting for a moment before washing their hands for a quick midday meal.

'Ready?' Gumi called out after lunch.

Off they went, back to the field to resume their toil for a few hours more. As the afternoon sun bore down on their backs, I could see that their energy was on the wane. But they did not stop until dusk when Gumi signalled with these words:

'Time to stop. Let's go home.'

Everyone bore a tired smile as she trudged back to Gumi's courtyard. Caked with mud all over, the women took turns to rinse their hands and feet. They hung around, chatting happily while waiting for supper. The day's work was done but they had only covered half of Gumi's rice field. Tomorrow would be another day.

'How is it that your friends help out so willingly?' I asked Gumi after she finished clearing the dishes.

'These friends and I have been helping each other for the last few years,' she said. 'We work together as a group when it is planting time. We started with my farm this year. After we have finished, we will move on to her farm,' she said, pointing to the woman who had been helping her with the dishes. 'It takes us two to three days to finish planting each field. We should be done with all our farms before month's end. To us, this is work exchange. They help me plant my field and I help each of them in return. It is much faster working as a group like that.'

'Do you ever lose count of the help you have received or the help you have to give in return?' I asked Gumi.

'Never!' said the woman who had never spent a day in school. 'We always remember everything, no matter how long ago the help was given or received. We never make a mistake.'

Needless to say I was impressed by the sense of community evident in this innovative method of exchanging labour in kind. Not knowing if this was unique to the Mosuos, it did remind me of a contrasting episode when I visited my grandfather's village in the south of China some years back.

I had arrived during the planting season and gamely agreed to go with some women from the village to put rice saplings to soil on a neighbouring farm. The women dressed me in boots and gloves before I joined them in the wet field. Far from helping out on a work-exchange programme, we did it for money. I was paid 20 yuan for slogging it out that afternoon.

The community spirit among the Mosuos is so strong that at times help is given willingly and spontaneously, without any accounting or reckoning. On driving to Gumi's in Baju village during one New Year celebration, I witnessed a commotion of people shouting and running with empty pails in their hands. I looked to where they were headed and was shocked to see a roaring fire gutting a house nearby. I stopped and joined the throng.

The villagers had already formed a water-pail line, the ones by a pond filling up buckets with water and passing the pails along to the person up the line, all the way to the burning house. Those at the end of the line poured water from the buckets on the burning house, then threw them down.

On seeing a gap in the make-do operation, I jumped in, retrieving two empty pails and running back to the pond to hand them over to the water fillers. Dozens of us worked ceaselessly for close to an hour before the fire was finally put under control.

Only then did the fire engine from town make an appearance. We stopped momentarily, grateful that help was finally at hand. We watched as the firefighters tried and tried but failed to get the water pump working. Nothing happened, no water came rushing through the hose. As if directed by an unseen conductor, we immediately went back to what we were doing and continued the communal firefighting effort until the flames were finally doused.

Watching the entire village of Baju pitching in to put out the fire was awe-inspiring. I was further moved to learn that the village head had sent out word the same day to encourage every home to contribute cash and kind to the stricken family. This was truly community spirit with its best face on.

Pitching in as a community takes a heavy toll. Because the individual lives of the villagers are so closely intertwined in the life of the community, every family is expected, even obliged, to participate and lend a hand in every event and happening. For every baby's first full moon, every child's coming-of-age, each blessing of a new home and each funeral in the village, every family is compelled socially to send at least one person to attend and contribute to the joint pool of volunteer helpers, without whom no event would take off.

Community spirit has a strange way of metamorphosing into community property. I have read about ancient societies treating possessions as community property rather than recognizing them as the private property of individuals. While I understand the concept on an intellectual level, it was something else when I came face to face with it in real life.

I think the first time it struck me was seeing Gumi running over to a neighbour to 'borrow' two bags of salt. Another time, I witnessed a friend walking over to his uncle's house and helping himself to a load of charcoal because he needed it for a barbeque at home. He did this without asking anyone at home for permission. With charcoal in hand he turned around to walk home without as much as a backward glance.

Sometimes bigger things were treated as community property. In Gumi's house one day, a neighbour sauntered over and asked for the keys to the family's motorbike. He was going to town and needed transport to get there. Without flinching, Gizi handed over the keys. The neighbour promptly rode his bike away.

'You let him use your motorbike, just like that, no questions asked?' I asked incredulously.

'Yes, of course,' Gizi replied, implying that it never occurred to him to refuse such a request.

'I would do the same to him too!' he added.

So I came to understand that the concept of communal property extended to things small and big, from a bagful of salt to a motorbike. So far so good, as I observed how the logic of communal property worked in practice among the Mosuos. At this stage, I was still an observer on an abstract level.

Reality hit home when the concept was imposed on me directly. It had to do with the new four-wheel-drive SUV I bought for my use around Lugu Lake. The car had served me well, zipping along treacherous mountain roads and slippery mud paths in the lake region.

When I decamped from Lugu Lake for extended periods, I would leave the car behind, entrusting the keys to a good friend. I simply assumed that the keys would be used to start the car now and then. I thought nothing of it until someone else reported to me that he had seen my friend driving the car around town. Before I took leave the second time, I decided to impose more specific restrictions on the use of the car.

'Only you can drive it. No one else!' I said, adding, 'Please do not use the car to ferry tourists around the lake as my insurance does not cover that.'

'No problem,' he replied, taking over the keys.

Reassured, I thought no more about the arrangement. On my return, I found to my horror that different people had been seen driving my vehicle, all of them cruising around the lake with carloads of tourists. The friend with my car keys not only ferried tourists in the car but also let his friends use it, in the way he would have done if the car had been his own. He treated it as community property and completely ignored my instructions.

These episodes really riled me even though I tried hard to accept the concept of community property on a personal and emotional level. To my Mosuo friend, any restriction on the use of someone's property would be selfish and not in tune with his entrenched sense of community property. I found out to my dismay that no matter how hard I tried to internalize this casual attitude to personal property, I could not exorcise the close attachment I felt to my own possessions. After so many years in Lugu Lake, it still stings viscerally whenever someone takes any of my possessions without my express consent.

Knowing I simply could not bring myself to embrace the Mosuo attitude on community property, I finally sold my car to Zhaxi. For a discounted price, he agreed to let me have use of the car for the duration of my stays there.

Getting to know the Mosuos in juxtaposition to Chinese society invariably leads me back to things matriarchal. Walking into a Mosuo home is another and most crucial lesson in the female scheme of things. I learnt my lesson when I first set foot into a matrilineal home. A young woman I had given a lift to invited me in when I dropped her at her home in a village next to Gumi's.

She guided me to the grandmother's room in her house where she introduced me to an elderly woman and two young women. They were all seated on floor cushions by the side of the grandmother's wooden bed. I smiled at the elder as she tended to the fire in the hearth.

'Hello, my name is Ah Hong and I am from Singapore visiting Lugu Lake,' I said.

'How are you? Our family name is Aha,' she said, while taking a puff of her cigarette. 'Please sit down and have a cup of tea,' she added, pointing to a cushion on the other side of the hearth.

Soon an elderly man came limping in supported by a younger man. They joined me on the side of the room facing the row of women on the opposite side. I could hear the voices of at least four young teenagers in the courtyard outside.

Not knowing any better and more by habit than anything else, I mentally identified the Aha family members by resorting to my understanding of a normal Chinese nuclear family. In this large family, there apparently was an elderly grandfather, his wife the grandmother, three daughters, among whom one was married to the younger man, with the other two daughters remaining single, plus the four children who were the offspring of the married couple. What puzzled me was that the number of children exceeded the mandated two-child-per-rural-household rule in China (the equivalent rule for a family in the big cities being one child per couple). This family, I thought, had more than its permitted share of children born to a nuclear family.

But I was in the land of the Mosuos with its unique matriarchal roots. The Aha family was a 'matrilineal big family', as the Mosuos would call it, and the rules of a patriarchal nuclear family did not apply.

I was wrong to see this family through the prism of a traditional patriarchal family setup. This perspective may be relevant in contemporary China, where a three-generation family consists of a one-man-one-wife grandparent pair in the first generation, their son and his wife in the second generation, and the children born to the son-wife pair in the third generation, based on the inviolate dogma that the man of the house traces the bloodline of his family up through his male ancestral side and down paternally via his sons and daughters, and the sons and daughters born only of his sons.

It dawned on me that I was trying to fit a square patriarchal peg into a round matriarchal hole. The Aha family inhabits a world that is wholly different from and in direct contrast to the world defined by male dominance. Their family structure inhabits the flip side of the world with which we are familiar. I had to consciously flip the lens and re-imagine it from the other side if I were to understand just who made up the Aha household.

After reading many sociological tomes and after many conversations with my Mosuo friends, I know that at the very heart of it Mosuo culture is about matrilineal lineage. A Mosuo family simply consists of everyone related directly to the maternal bloodline of the central figure of a woman, the grandmother, based on the inviolate principle that she traces her bloodline up through her female ancestral side and down maternally via her daughters and sons, and the daughters and sons born only of her daughters.

The starting point is to imagine three links in the axis linking a three-generation matrilineal family. The link starts with the grandmother in the first generation. Her male siblings, born of her mother, may be included at this level under the grandmother-brother formula, as I call it. Her female siblings are usually excluded because each of these sisters would have formed her own matrilineal home.

The next link comprises all the children born to the grandmother in the second generation. This almost goes without saying. The grandmother gave birth to them and they have her bloodline. What is unusual under this grandmother-daughter/son combination is the total absence of any mention of the *axias* of her daughters or sons. The idea of any family member bringing into the family an *axia* is unimaginable because the *axia* bears a different maternal bloodline, having been born of another woman bearing a different maternal bloodline. Quite simply, an *axia* is a lover, someone with whom the daughter or the son has a sexual alliance, but the *axia* remains outside the matrilineal bloodline and never becomes family. A male *axia* 'visits' the woman in her home but does not stay to form any permanent liaison with her. This is a society without the concept of marriage, and so every adult family member is a 'single' person from our viewpoint.

The final link for the third generation consists of children born only to the daughters of the grandmother. This logic makes sense if we trace the matrilineal bloodline at this level. Only the daughters of the grandmother can carry the same maternal bloodline on to the next generation. In the third generation, both girls and boys born to a daughter of the grandmother belong to the grandmother's family because they have their mother's bloodline. Should the son of the grandmother beget a child with an outsider *axia*, that child's maternal bloodline would follow that of its mother, the *axia*, which is different from the son's original maternal bloodline. That child belongs to a different maternal bloodline and therefore a different family. That child does not count as part of the grandmother's family.

The key to understanding this grandmother-mother-daughter/son reference is that a child is considered by the Mosuos as solely the child of the mother, not her *axia*'s. The fact that the mother needed a male *axia* to become pregnant is irrelevant because the male factor does not impact on the grandmother's maternal lineage. Taking this to its logical conclusion, a Mosuo child in the third generation belongs to the mother's and the grandmother's maternal family.

The other key to remember is that the *axia* of each and every member of a Mosuo family is not accounted for at all in the composition of the family. *Axias* are never part of a traditional matrilineal family, not at the first generation where the grandmother is concerned, not at the second generation for any of the daughters or sons of the grandmother, and not at the third generation for every daughter or son of the grandmother's daughters.

Applying these maxims to work out just who is related to whom within the Aha family proved to be both challenging and revelatory for me.

Starting with the elderly woman smoking by the hearthside, I made my first educated guess.

'This is for you, grandmother,' I said as I presented a carton of cigarettes to the Aha matriarch, not anyone else.

'Thank you,' she said, confirming to me that she was indeed the grandmother in the Aha matrilineal family.

Without saying a word, she gave a look to the young woman I drove home. There was a slight glint of authority in grandmother's eyes. My new friend knew precisely what to do, walking over to the hearth for the hot water in the kettle to make tea for us. Like the rest of the family, she would never have dared to question the authority of the head of the household.

As befitting a matriarch, the Aha grandmother was ensconced at the top seat on the female, and therefore the more important, side of the grandmother's room where the grandmother's bed was situated. This side of the room was marked by the larger of the twin supporting pine pillars. The matriarchal symbolism does not escape me. I knew to greet her first as the chief elder of the family.

'Meet my older brother,' she said as I turned to the elderly man who sat across the hearth from the grandmother. She had just confirmed my understanding of the grandmother-brother link. Because no *axia* is a family member, the elderly man could not have been her *axia*. And because he must be related to her through her maternal bloodline, he had to be her brother. Although he sat on the less important 'male' side of the room marked by the smaller pine pillar, his occupying the top seat on his side meant that he was the highest-ranking male in the family.

'Meet the rest of my family,' grandmother said, indicating the four young people in the room.

'Hello, Gumi,' I said, using the polite Mosuo term meaning 'younger sister' taught to me by Ladzu's mother, as each of the three young women smiled at me in turn.

I was betting that all three of them were the daughters of the Aha grandmother. I had a hunch that this was the correct conclusion, based on the grandmother-daughter/son link for the second generation of the Ahas. They were 'single' women, no husbands in tow.

As no *axia* is a family member, none of the three women could be the *axia* of the young man who sat by his elderly uncle. On his part and for the same reason, the young man himself could not be the *axia* of any of the daughters. He too is a single man. Having the same maternal bloodline, he had to be the son of the grandmother and brother to the three sisters.

'Hi, kids,' I said as I handed red packets of money to the three girls and the youngest teenage boy in the courtyard. I assumed they were variously the children of grandmother's daughters, using the third grandmother-mother-daughter/son link. Only children, both girls and boys, born of grandmother's daughters would have their grandmother's bloodline flowing in their veins. They could not have been the issue of the Aha son because, as a male, he would be unable to pass on his mother's bloodline.

'Please tell me which of the youngsters are your children,' I asked the three Aha sisters later. They did, bearing out my hunch. I guess they would be viewed as single mothers in contemporary China. These same children addressed the adult son of the Aha grandmother as 'Uncle', further corroborating my deduction that the children were the maternal nieces and nephews of the Aha son.

After a great deal of struggle with the intricate maze posed by the Mosuo matrilineal family structure, I was pleased with my effort. I had cracked the Aha family mystery. I knew I had finally arrived at a place in my grey matter that would do me well in unravelling the social obscurities of this mountain tribe.

As the whole picture of the Aha family emerged, I wondered at the unique and quite radical way in which Mosuo society organizes itself around the feminine construct. Everything, it seems, begins and ends with the female at its crux. With all its complexities, it is entirely different from, and not seen elsewhere in, patriarchal societies.

I suppose in appreciating the logic inherent in the female-centric world of the Mosuos, I can take a step back and regard the patriarchal world of the Chinese as having its own logic too. Either type of society has its own internal gender-biased rationale. Each social system works in preserving the power that it chooses to value. Perhaps the almost universal patriarchal model has more appeal in the world, but if I were given the choice I would opt for the Mosuo matrilineal alternative.

5

Becoming
the Godmother

Unbeknownst to me, becoming a godmother to a Mosuo girl led me on a curious journey to becoming godmother of an entire village.

Being a Ganma is not new to me or to my cultural heritage – godmothers are commonplace in Chinese society. My first encounter with this practice occurred when I accompanied my mother and younger sister to the house of an elderly teacher who knew my mother. I still recall standing by and watching with interest when my sister was presented to the teacher and made to call her 'Ganma'. Her new godmother nodded seriously and gave her a red packet of money in acknowledgement of the formal recognition. My mother told us afterwards that my sister, who fell sick too often, would enjoy a change of luck by calling someone else mother.

When Ladzu acknowledged me as her godmother, I was already a veteran in things godmotherly. A few good girlfriends have over the years asked me to be godmother to their children, not so much to change their luck but to express their trust in me to do the right thing should anything happen to them. I was a godmother many times over and in all cases took my parenting seriously.

However, I did not plan to do this in a big way when I moved to Lugu Lake. Events progressed slowly. I got to know new friends at the same lazy pace I took to settle in to my new Mosuo home. Over time, the family members of my friends became friends in turn, enlarging my circle of acquaintances. Before I knew it, I was juggling a busy social calendar.

Most times, friends would casually invite me over for dinner with little advance notice. At other times, Ladzu would ring, asking me to go along with her and her brother for a lark, whether it was picking apples or mushrooms. Never one to turn down an invitation, I would almost always accept each summons, alternating my visits between new and old friends.

Gumi came to be the constant in my social life. Hers would be the first and last meal I attended on each visit. In between, she never failed to drag me along on shopping trips to the market and to each and every social event in her village. My immediate network of friends widened when she introduced me to her large family.

'I am the youngest in a family of eight sisters and brothers,' Gumi said quite early on in our friendship. 'I have a mother who lives in her own house very near to mine. You must meet her.'

'A Ma' (the Mosuo term Gumi used for her mother) was in her declining years when I met her. She had met her tall, dark and handsome *axia* while still a sweet young thing living in her maternal home. Her *axia* came to visit her often in her matrilineal home and, consistent with Mosuo tradition, she carried on a walking marriage arrangement with him. This was not so much a marriage as the Mosuo way for her *axia* to spend the nights with her, then return back to his maternal home in the mornings.

In the course of their relatively long-term liaison, which did not require them to get married, she gave birth to four boys and a girl. The children were hers, not her *axia*'s.

But for a quirk in Mosuo history, she might have continued to invite her *axia*, or a new *axia*, to visit her. In the 1960s the new central government in China had been in place for more than a decade. The Communist Party leadership had by then rolled out its land redistribution policies even in far-flung Yunnan, which would have explained how it was that A Ma had her own piece of land. There was, however, scant official intervention in the social practices of a small minority like the Mosuos, who continued with their ancient matriarchal ways and marriage-less form of family structure just as they did under a millennium of imperial Chinese rule.

Change came overnight when the Cultural Revolution rolled across the country. The Red Guards of the Revolution made their way to remote Lugu Lake with a mandate to wipe out all vestiges of feudal social practices. On discovering that the Mosuos had sexual partners without marrying them, they denounced the age-old Mosuo practice as barbaric and primitive.

The political message was clear. They decreed that all Mosuos had to break off from the archaic walking marriage and adopt the modern civilized form of legal marriage, committing the one-man-one-wife pair to a permanent union. In one stroke, they imposed two radical deviations from the tribal norm. Marriage was made compulsory, so was monogamy.

The Mosuos were persuaded, pressured and later coerced into entering into monogamous marriages in those turbulent times. Like many other young people with *axia* partners, A Ma and her man were caught up in the maelstrom and found themselves declared wife and husband without much ado.

'My mother left her matrilineal home to set up a new home in Baju

71

with my father as a married couple. My brothers and sister went along,' Gumi told me. 'Later she gave birth to two more brothers before having me, the youngest child. We are eight altogether.'

Having to feed so many young and hungry mouths at their small farm holding was tough for A Ma and her *axia*-turned-husband.

'Sometimes my father had to go on long journeys as a *mabang* (stable hand) on the tea-horse trail to earn extra grain and meat for the family,' Gumi added. 'Because we were so poor, my mother "gave away" two of my older brothers and my only sister to relatives. She also sent Zhaxi away to a Tibetan Buddhist lamasery.'

Struggling in their hand-to-mouth existence, A Ma and her husband could ill afford to send their children to school. Only one of her sons went to school for a couple of years, another son learnt to read and write at the lamasery. All the other six children were illiterate, like most of the Mosuo population of that generation growing up in the poverty-stricken days of the 1960s, 1970s and 1980s.

Being illiterate does not seem to handicap Gumi and her siblings. Having met all of them, I can vouch for the fact that each is coping well to varying degrees in their changing world. Seeing Gumi use her handphone is proof enough. While she is unable to read the names in her contact list, which is recorded in Chinese with the help of Gizi, she eyes the telephone numbers as she scrolls through the list and unfailingly zooms in on the correct number for the person she wishes to call. This is because she has memorized the last four digits of the telephone number of each of her friends.

Illiterate though they may be, everyone in Gumi's generation speaks Mandarin, having learnt it the only way they know how, as an oral language. With a smattering of the spoken Chinese language, they each get by in their daily lives when they interact with those outside their community.

Through the years, I got to know A Ma and some of Gumi's siblings and their children really well, close enough to be considered part of that big family. My life in Lugu Lake revolves first and foremost around them.

Gumi's brother number six, Jizuo, is a buddy of mine. He was the Man Friday at the horse farm when I moved into my cottage by Moon Lake, taking care of everything around the farm, including my house. If I had a leaky water faucet, he would appear with a wrench to fix it in no time. He would be the first to carry my heavy luggage or a heavy gas canister for my stove. Having green fingers, he would prune the roses and chrysanthemums growing in front of my terrace. Being illiterate did not stop him being a jack of all trades.

'I once worked as a horse trainer in a fancy equestrian school in the city,' he said proudly, while sharing with me another one of his wise homespun philosophies on life.

One winter night in my darkened dining room during an electricity outage, I had choked on a chicken bone. In desperation I called Jizuo.

'Buxin le!' I croaked. I meant, roughly, 'It is hopeless', but to him it meant I was about to die. He dropped the phone and ran a full kilometre to save my life. He knows full well I shall forever be indebted to him.

With his *axia*, Jizuo has two grown-up daughters, the elder of whom, Ercher, is a winsome young woman whom I got close to from the many dinners with her family. She has two little ones, a much-reduced number than during her father's generation, before the change in the Chinese family-planning policy restricted the number to two per rural family and one per city family.

When she had the last baby, she asked me an unexpected question.

'Would you please be a Ganma to my baby girl?'

I was surprised. Perhaps my godparenting skills with regard to

73

her cousin, Ladzu, as well as her own younger sister, Xiaomei, had impressed her. The headcount of my godchildren was growing. I was made to accept another unlikely candidate when a 40-something male cousin of Ladzu insisted that he too qualified as a godson. He continues to address me as Ganma.

Of course, Ladzu was the first of my Mosuo godchildren. When I first knew her, she was in junior high school. Very soon after, I noticed that both she and her younger brother did their homework squatting on the floor, their books and pens perched on makeshift stools serving as tabletops. My first gift to them was a table big enough for two so that they could study in comfort. My next purchases were supplementary textbooks and other reading material.

I discovered too that Ladzu loved to dance. At the slightest prompt she would jump up and put on a performance, dancing a mix of ethnic styles in time to tunes played on her father's mobile phone. She reminded me of myself at ten wanting to be the next Margot Fonteyn. Having asked around, I found out that the prestigious Yunnan Arts Institute in Kunming was about to hold dance auditions for new students in the coming spring.

'Would you be interested in trying for a place in a dance school?' I asked the 15-year-old.

'Yes, yes!' came her quick reply.

Springing into action, I had her father build a makeshift wooden *barre* at home for the first ballet lesson I was about to give her. I dredged up forgotten moves from my memory to show the young girl the five classic ballet positions and some other dance exercises.

Together we choreographed two items for her upcoming audition, one a typical Mosuo dance and the other a Tibetan-style number. I made her practise each time I visited, playing the stern dance teacher all the while.

1. A Mosuo matriarch such as this one always takes her prime place on the more important female side of the room by the family hearth, where the embers are never allowed to die out.

2. Each Mosuo homestead slaughters one to two home-bred pigs in late autumn, salts and spices the meat, and lets it hang on wooden poles to dry and serve as the meat supply through the cold winter months.

3. This is the first scene that greets me in the morning as I look out from the terrace of my Mosuo cottage to the massif known as Gemu Mountain Goddess, the grand old deity of the Mosuo people.

4. Self-assured Mosuo women dressed in their festive finery taking up their positions to perform at the annual Gemu Mountain Goddess Festival, held in high summer in honour of their favourite deity.

5. The heavy summer downpour does not deter these Mosuo women and men ready to kick into their *jiachuo*, the circle dance round a bonfire, during the Gemu Mountain Goddess Festival.

6. All dressed up attending the Gemu Festival are Erchima (left), my comrade in arms for non-stop partying, me in the middle, and Big Sister (right), the elder sister of Gumi, the mother of my two godchildren.

7. A Ma, the grandmother of my godchildren and the matriarch of my adoptive family of Gumi and her seven siblings. This picture of her whiling away the afternoon in her courtyard was taken one year before her funeral.

8. The macho Mosuo peacocks strutting their stuff at the Gemu Mountain Goddess Festival.

9. My Mosuo home under construction, directed by Zhaxi, the uncle of my godchildren, who planned, designed and executed the building in nine months.

10. The multi-hued and much decorated 'grandmother's room' in my typical Mosuo home. Of particular note are the fine wood-carved detailing and colourful ceiling painted Sistine Chapel style with the painter on his back on the scaffolding.

11. Ladzu, my goddaughter (taller one, second right), and her teenage friends all dolled up in formal ethnic wear to celebrate the Spring Festival in the hamlet of Baju, the hometown of Ladzu's mother, Gumi.

12. The first Mosuo matriarch I met in Lugu Lake when I was taken to view her 300-year-old traditional Mosuo home built entirely of pine logs.

13. The humble, unassuming shrine built to honour the Mosuos' favourite deity, Gemu Mountain Goddess, the site of the annual Gemu Festival enacted to thank the goddess for being their guardian.

14. A portrait of three Mosuo women snapped during the annual Gemu Festival.

15. Tibetan Buddhist lamas chanting funeral rites before the burning pyre of a dearly departed, held at a makeshift site up on the mountainside.

16. Zhaxi, reputedly the 'Prince of Walking Marriages' or the Don Juan of Don Juans, also the uncle of my godchildren and the builder of my Mosuo home.

Audition time came too soon. I took Ladzu on her first plane ride to Kunming and barely made it in time to catch the last audition slot. Under the scrutiny of a most unfriendly dance teacher, Ladzu was first made to strike some dance poses before she launched into her first routine. She was nervous, to say the least, but she tried her best to execute the right moves.

'Tsk, tsk!' said the teacher before she had finished. 'You are too stiff. Your shoulders are not pliable and your backbone is not flexible enough. At 15 you have left it too late to be a dancer!'

At that very moment, all our hopes were dashed. We were both feeling mightily dejected on leaving the audition hall. I could find few words of comfort for her. If only I had met Ladzu a couple of years earlier, I thought to myself, things might have ended up differently. She could have turned out to be the dancer I never became.

That failed dream was not the only setback for my goddaughter. A year later she failed her junior high-school examination and could not go on to high school. Everyone joined in the panic. Gumi thought it was time for Ladzu to go out to work.

'You can join the song and dance troupe at the Lige Performance Hall,' she told her daughter.

Ladzu's father had a different suggestion.

'You can go to a vocational nursing school. At least you will learn a trade,' he said.

'What do you want to do?' I asked my goddaughter.

She looked at us bewildered. She had no idea.

Not wanting to give up, I looked around for other alternatives. Within a day someone found me a tourism course in a vocational institute in Baoshan town not too far away from Lugu Lake. I convened a family conference in my house and spoke about the two options open to Ladzu, either to take up nursing or train in the hotel and restaurant trade. Nursing, I said, required serious study and a strong stomach. Learning hospitality skills would be easier and provide plenty of career opportunities in Lugu Lake's burgeoning tourist industry.

'Make your decision, Ladzu,' her parents urged her.

'I think the tourism course,' she said finally after a few long minutes.

After assuring everyone that I would see to her fees and expenses during the first year and split the costs with her parents for the remainder of the four-year course, I told them there was no time to waste. Applicants were due to be interviewed in two days. The journey to Baoshan would take a whole day of driving and we had to set out the very next day.

Everything went well after we got there. Ladzu passed the interview with flying colours and was admitted as a student. That was three years ago. Ladzu is now in her final year and has begun her practical training in a five-star hotel in Lijiang.

My goddaughter was not the only 'relative' I had helped through school. When I met Xiaomei, the younger sister of Ercher and daughter of Gumi's brother Jizuo, she was already a second-year student at a university in Baoshan and the first among the children of Gumi's siblings to go to university. Bright and hardworking, she was on a part-grant, part-scholarship from a German foundation to study tourism management. She topped her class in her freshman year. At times when her schooling expenses ran over, I would help.

Xiaomei gained her degree in tourism studies *summa cum laude*, once more taking the top spot in her graduating class. She now works as a licensed tourist guide in a famous hot-spring town in Yunnan province near the Burmese border.

Although not formally a goddaughter, Xiaomei had always looked up to me as a mentor.

Xiaomei and Ladzu, along with the younger generations in Lugu

Lake, are far luckier than their parents' generation. They get to attend school, something not available to their parents. But it is gratifying to note that schooling has reached the outermost regions in China, where it is compulsory for every child in a population of 1.4 billion to complete primary school. There remains a gap in education between rural China and the urban areas. Chinese cities big and small can boast of a long history of education and literacy, and while the policy-makers of the new China have been pushing for universal schooling, it has taken much longer for it to take root in these hidden mountains.

Still, going to school for a Mosuo kid is no easy task, quite different from a Beijing or Shanghai child in more pampered circumstances. Schools in the Mosuo highlands are few and far between, and not just around the corner or down the road. There is only one primary school for every two to three hamlets, and just one junior high school in the main town of Yongning to service all the villages this side of Lugu Lake. There are no school buses, so most junior-high students have to lodge in the cramped dormitories.

My godson either walked or hitched a ride on his friend's bicycle to his primary school almost eight kilometres from home. On Sunday afternoons my goddaughter would start out on foot from home to reach the school dormitory one-and-a-half hours away, where she would literally bunk in two to a single bed, 24 to each hostel room.

Unlike Xiaomei, who made it to university, a lot of Mosuo teenagers fall through the cracks in the education system. Xiaomei's older cousins grew up in more trying economic times during the 1990s. Although they attended school, they only managed as far as junior high school, if that. Her sister Ercher, the mother of my new godchild, had to leave home to join an ethnic performing troupe in the nearby tourist town of Dali after finishing junior high. Her two oldest cousins, Zhashi and Mao Niu, the sons of the eldest brother of Gumi, make their living driving heavy trucks. Other cousins of my godchildren's generation who dropped out of school early make do with working as waiters and chefs.

Even so, the third generation of A Ma's grandchildren are educated and literate, able to double up as translators for their parents and act as their reading eyes and writing hands.

A Ma's grandchildren have spawned a fourth generation of great-grandchildren, little babies and toddlers including my new goddaughter. They are the fortunate generation. Having been born in the last decade to parents who are beginning to reap the benefits of tourism, they are pandered to in a way their parents would never have dreamt possible. These kids wear new clothes and new shoes, unlike their grandparents in Gumi's generation who grew up in tattered old rags and ran about barefoot. They are continually being showered with presents bought from department stores in the city while their parents had to make do with crude handmade toys. The world will be their oyster as they grow up in the twenty-first century.

My presence as a Ganma collecting godchildren in Gumi's family was slowly gaining attention in Baju village. It did not help that Gumi insisted on introducing me as Ganma everywhere we went. Stories about Ladzu's godmother helping her through school began to spread and, before long, villagers were coming up to me to commend me on my efforts.

Duojie, my lama friend and self-appointed do-gooder around the village, must have heard the news too. He approached me one day about a bright teenage student from Yongning who was struggling to pay his way as a boarder at the only high school serving the Lugu Lake region, located more than 120 kilometres away.

'Would you consider financing his living expenses in his final year at the high school?' Duojie asked me, adding, 'I believe this student is smart enough and has every chance of passing his university entrance examination.'

The amount he mentioned seemed insubstantial, so I readily agreed. This student turned out to be my best investment to date, making good his examination the following year and gaining a place in a good university in the province. I continue to help in paying part of his university living expenses.

I chalked up more karma when I started helping another young woman who came out top in the provincial list of minority high-school students taking the same national college entrance examination, called *gaokao* in Chinese. This nationwide examination is the modern-day version of the ancient Chinese imperial system of examination open to everyone to test their mettle against the best brains in the country. If successful, the candidates in imperial China would have been rewarded with life-long high service in the national bureaucracy. Their contemporary counterparts gain admittance to universities of their choice.

My best claim to fame among the Mosuo community had yet to surface. Here I return to the beginning of my story about Gemu, the iconic deity of the Mosuo people, and the festival of Zhuanshanjie held in homage to the Mountain Goddess. The annual festival has been around for hundreds of years, if not longer, but has dwindled in importance in recent times as old practices make way for new.

Since my first time at the Goddess Festival, I had privately lamented the dwindling number of participants in the annual event. Zhuanshanjie for me was a jolly, crowded, community event that first time round. Filled with local colour, the festival drew scores of women, men and children from the many Mosuo villages and hamlets around Lugu Lake. Tibetan Buddhist lamas of the Gelupa Yellow Hat sect chanted in a tent on one side while their religious counterparts, the Sakya Red Hat sect, conducted worship in a small temple on the other. In the middle of it all, Gemu's shrine beckoned young and old celebrants to pay tribute to their pagan past. Enthusiastic villagers who dressed up cavorted in full dance, completing a magnificently eye-catching Mosuo tableau.

Roll forward to the following year and I saw the number of merry-makers dwindle to half. Of those who attended the festival, few had bothered to dress up in their festive gear. A small group tried valiantly to get the dancing going but there was scant interest. A few stragglers stayed to build picnic fires. The crowd, small to begin with, petered out early. When I mounted my horse to go home round midday, there was hardly a soul left.

It was a much smaller and sadder gathering the third summer I returned for the festival. A mere handful of worshippers, dressed in their everyday clothes, made their way to pray at the Gemu shrine, only to come down the slope to an empty fairground. There was no ceremony, no music, no dance, no picnic. Almost a non-event as far as I could see. Nobody lingered. The festival was all over in less than an hour.

'What happened to this year's event?' I said aloud to no one in particular, not believing what I had witnessed.

'The local authorities have stopped supporting the event,' someone muttered next to me. 'They decided it was not worthwhile. This is no festival at all.'

I felt let down. This was the most important event in the Mosuo calendar and yet it seemed like a dying patient in its last throes of life. It was a sad day for the older folk, who must have been devastated by the insult to their collective memory of what had always been a joyous highpoint in their social year. It was sadder still for the young ones, who would grow up oblivious to the meaning of being Mosuo. Perhaps saddest of all would be the Goddess herself, who was becoming a forgotten icon of yesteryear.

The sombre mood I felt led to an epiphanous moment for me. If no one else was going to keep the Gemu Festival alive, then I would do something about it. I would not let this unique Mosuo cultural vestige disappear.

Putting on my lawyer hat, I came up with what I thought was a brilliant plan to revive Zhuanshanjie. I needed to persuade a notable local to spearhead a sponsorship drive to fund the festival. Zhaxi, my builder and apparently a man of influence, was my obvious choice.

'How about going with me to talk to the hoteliers and restaurateurs in Lige and ask each of them to donate, say, 500RMB so that we can collect enough to fund the festival next year?' I asked him, convinced that the amount mentioned, a little more than £50, was a piddling sum to any business.

'There are at least 30 to 40 hotels and restaurants in this place which depend on the tourist trade, and supporting Zhuanshanjie will surely boost tourism. Thirty times 500RMB will give us enough money for next year's Mountain Goddess Festival,' I added.

He listened patiently to me, but his eyes betrayed a less than lukewarm reception.

'I don't think we can get enough support,' he said meekly. From his lack of enthusiasm, I suspected that even he was not willing to stump up his share of what was really a small amount in the grand scheme of things.

'So much for a brilliant idea,' I told myself as I walked away, dejected.

But I was not one to give up so easily. I kept a keen eye on the lunar calendar, and two months before the date of the festival, I made a decision to take matters into my own hands. Having made the acquaintance of a retired Mosuo teacher, Zhiba Zhashi, who in his own time volunteers as a cultural custodian at all the local events, I phoned him and asked if we could meet to discuss something important. I had a hunch that he would be the right person for the job I was about to propose.

'Would you be interested in organizing this year's Mountain Goddess Festival if I were to give some money for it?' I asked when we met.

'What do you mean?' he asked. 'Do you mean you are willing to pay for the expenses of the festival?'

'Yes, I mean exactly that,' I said, half hoping that the expenses would not amount to too much.

'Would 5,000RMB do?' Just £500 really.

'Hmm, 5,000RMB. It may be possible if we are not too ambitious to make it a big event,' he said.

'We cannot just let the festival die off,' I pleaded.

After a few nervous minutes for me, he smiled.

'All right. I will do it. Let's do it!'

He turned out to be the right choice after all. As one committed to preserving the Mosuo culture, he understood the meaning of what I was proposing. He, like me, wanted to keep the festival alive.

I was elated and happy to leave things to him, only making a few suggestions of what could be added to the day's programme. He showed me his plans a few days later. They looked fine.

Zhiba Zhashi sprang into action, making the rounds and speaking to the village heads around Lugu Lake, spreading the word that there would after all be a festival that year. He dangled a straw – there would be singing and dancing contests and participants would be handed small tokens of cash in red packets. Within days, we heard back that five hamlets had signed up to take part. We were excited. The festival would take place after all!

On the morning of the festival I made a point of arriving early on horseback. As I rode in I saw to my surprise the fairground teeming with crowds of people. Many of them had come dressed in full Mosuo costume. As I looked around I saw groups of locals dressed in different colours to show that they represented particular villages. They added a festive air to the crowd that was slowly gathering in the background. Soon, people hastened about, looking for a good spot to pitch their family tents and start their cooking fires. This time round the crowd was much bigger and the atmosphere jollier than the previous couple of years. It was looking good.

The cultural custodian outdid himself by kicking off the festival with a show-stopper. A deep gong sounded, and an imposing-looking Mosuo *daba* in his full shaman regalia called everyone to attention. He intoned over the microphone the familiar traditional call to Gemu, the Mountain Goddess, and set alight a pile of pine branches.

'We wish you a happy day, our beloved Gemu Mountain Goddess,' the *daba* chanted, flicking holy spring water into the air. 'Let the festival begin!'

'But first things first,' Zhiba Zhashi announced, taking over the microphone. 'Our festival would not have been possible without the warm and enthusiastic support of a Singaporean friend of the Mosuo people.'

Signalling me forward, he ceremoniously presented me with a yellow *hadaq*. I accepted the holy scarf and began haltingly to repeat two simple sentences in Mosuo that I had rehearsed all morning.

'Hello, my Mosuo friends. I hope you all enjoy yourselves today as we celebrate Gemu on Zhuanshanjie.'

The familiar sight of the pied piper flautist appeared and the first group of dancers from a village next to Baju strutted over to centre stage to start the dance contest. The dancing went on as each village dance troupe tried to outperform their rivals. Handphone cameras clicked and tourist video-cams zoomed in on the action. A singing contest followed the dancing, and from a handful of contestants, a middle-aged woman from Baju with a piercing voice who sang a favourite local song *a capella* was declared the winner.

The Baju crowd went wild with applause. The village head came over and patted me on the back.

However, disaster struck the following year. The Mosuo community was reeling from the first earthquake in living memory, just two months before the festival. Almost down to the last log home, every homestead had suffered some degree of damage from the quake which measured nearly six on the Richter scale. Although only one person died and a couple more were injured, many of my friends were still staying in emergency rescue tents pitched in their courtyards next to their damaged homes.

'There is no money for the festival again,' Zhiba Zhashi said when I asked him. 'The officials are distracted by the bad news.'

I heard rumours floating about, with people believing that Gemu had been so frightened by the earthquake, which caused a large permanent crack down her middle, that she had fled and abandoned the community.

'All the more, we must hold the festival,' I said to Zhiba Zhashi. 'We have to restore the faith of the people that Gemu has not left them. It doesn't matter that there is no government money. We can do it again. I will double last year's sponsorship.'

Together we worked harder than before, expanding the programme to include two more *dabas* to inaugurate the opening, and local primary school children to perform and recite the Gemu Mountain Goddess story. This time I rehearsed a longer Mosuo speech.

'Gemu Goddess, if you have really gone away after the earthquake, we invite you back today. Come back to where you belong. Come back to the embrace of your people. Come back to protect us all.'

To this day I continue to carry the Gemu event. If I am lucky to have supportive friends from Singapore or Beijing join me at the festival, I impose a small goddess tax on them to help finance the event.

I suppose my fan club grew year by year as people learnt of my sponsorship. In some way, they might even have interpreted it as a motherly gesture. I would like to believe that my undertakings as a godmother and a friend of the Mosuo have by now qualified me as an insider. And this brings me back to the story of my starting out as the godmother of one to becoming the village godmother of one and all.

I was already 'Ganma' to those who knew me in Gumi's village. However, I did not realize how widespread this usage had become until one day two strangers yelled out to me in the big city of Lijiang.

'Ganma! Ganma!!'

I looked around and found an elderly couple whom I did not recognize waving at me. They repeated 'Ganma' from across the street. I waved back. They came forward with the widest grins.

'Ganma, fancy seeing you here,' the woman said.

'Hello,' I responded, finally getting it that the couple must have come from Gumi's village.

'And what are you doing in this big place so far from Baju?' I asked to confirm my suspicion.

'We just arrived here to see the doctor. See you back in Baju soon, Ganma,' they said in parting.

The penny dropped. I had finally arrived. I had become the godmother of an entire Mosuo village!

6

Hunting and Eating
in Bygone Times

For one used to buying vegetables and meat all neatly cut up, washed and packed in mega supermarkets in Beijing, each of my food experiences in the Lugu Lake highlands transports me to a bygone era inconceivable in modern Chinese life.

The main philosophy in Mosuo cuisine is simple, in a land where simplicity is possible only if we go back in time. Eat what you can find and, if not, grow your own. The Mosuos carry on a rudimentary form of subsistence, gathering and hunting for edibles in the high pine forests, growing basic crops of rice, corn and potatoes and making do with simple animal husbandry, the aim being nothing more than to support the family. What they find or grow is seldom sold or bartered. Almost everything is done by hand or with simple tools that belong to another time.

These unsophisticated methods of sourcing food are an unusual throwback to an age long gone, probably in common with other pockets of minority communities living in remote parts of the country. Most of the rest of rural China has moved on to commercial or specialized farming in varying degrees, from small- and medium-sized holdings to large business farms.

How the Mosuo tribe goes about the business of food takes me back to the real basics, and it is from this modest starting point that the stuff of my food adventures begins.

I have seen and eaten many different and unusual foods but never been near a slaughterhouse before. An invitation from Gumi to witness a pig slaughter festival at her farm got me intrigued.

Every year around late autumn, the Mosuos celebrate the pig in all its glory in a frenzied post-harvest festival. It is not really a festival where everyone comes together to hold a community event, but a time when each homestead holds its own fête, killing and preserving pig meat from sows fattened on the farm.

Gumi had been building up to the festival long before issuing the invitation to me. Having harvested her potatoes, corn and rice and put them in storage, she and Gizi had finished the remaining chores of repairing farming tools and tidying up around the house. Activity on the farm had slowed down and as the days grew shorter and the autumnal sun grew dimmer, they were watching for signs of the weather changing from autumn to a near-winter chill.

Gumi called me just when the winds were starting to blow stronger and cooler with the air feeling more crisp and dry. Not bothering with a calendar, which she could not read anyway, she had spotted a sure sign that the time had come.

'I saw a few Tibetan black-necked cranes from the cold mountains in Tibet flying near my farm yesterday. This means winter is coming. It is time for our pig slaughter festival. Come over tomorrow!'

Hers was the first of at least half a dozen more invitations from other friends, eager to share their one chance in the year for a blowout.

When I got to Gumi's, the household was humming with activity. Everything was being prepared for the slaughter. Her sister came in with packets of salt, and her brother who lived down the road arrived with a large bag of spicy Sichuan flower pepper picked and dried from a tree in his backyard. Both ingredients were indispensable for curing the pork meat.

'How many pigs will be slaughtered today?' I asked Gumi.

'Two,' she said, pointing them out to Gizi and her brother. 'I have fed them for more than two years and put them on a fast for a week. They are ready for the kill.'

The two men rounded up the animals and trussed them in preparation for the slaughter. This was what I had come to witness. I would never get this opportunity in any city in China.

As Nongbu watched on the side while his father and uncle sharpened the knives for the big kill, I caught sight of Gumi and her sister walking away, reminding me of the Mosuo taboo against any killing by the women. Other than me and my camera, today's slaughtering was strictly a male affair.

Laying down a tarpaulin sheet in the centre of the courtyard, Gizi pulled pig number one on to the sheet and held it still. Mumbling a short prayer of thanks to the Harvest God, Gumi's brother gave a clean deep thrust with a sharpened wooden stake right to the heart of the animal. It was over almost instantly as the pig took only moments to be stilled.

Not being uneasy about killing for food, I did not flinch from seeing my first pig kill. I was more impressed with the way my Mosuo friends treated the slaughtering as a necessary something in the circle of life. They connected it to nature's bounty by calling up their pagan past, and I am sure they also connected it to a temporal break from the Buddhist admonition against the taking of life. And they honoured their unique tradition in keeping it away from the women.

Switching over to a knife, the butcher brother executed a deft stroke to slit the animal's throat. He positioned its neck over a large bowl to collect its still-warm blood. The men went on with their work, pouring boiling water over the carcass before scraping the hair off its skin. Gizi skilfully cut open the pig and used his bare hands to draw out the innards. Gumi's brother butchered the carcass into large pieces. It was only at that point, long after the final death throes had ended, that the women came back on the scene to take away the innards to be cleaned for sausage-making.

Continuing with their job, the men alternated between rubbing copious amounts of salt and pepper on the meat and chopping up the lean bits to use as stuffing for the sausages. Gizi handed Gumi the twin tenderloins of the pork to roast over the burning coals as everyone waited in anticipation of the well-done appetizer of tender meat.

'This will give us enough meat through the winter months,' Gumi told me as she supervised the men hanging the salted and spiced pork over a wooden pole under the eaves by the courtyard. Nothing went to waste in the best tradition of Mosuo head-to-tail eating as every part of the animal was preserved and hung to dry.

I waited for the last and my favourite part of the ritual. Gumi readied herself to make the most delicious black-pudding sausages, which to me were the centrepiece of the pork feast. Using a recipe handed down the ages, she placed piping hot rice moistened with a pan of steamy hot pork lard in a big vat and ladled the by-now coagulated pig blood on it, adding the seasoning. Then she dug in with her bare hands, kneading and turning the entire mixture over and over again until it turned a perfect mash of burgundy-coloured rice. Bloodied up to her forearms, she turned herself into a human sausage-making machine, with one hand holding the cleaned large intestines over a temporary holder fashioned out of a twig and the other hand stuffing the mixture into the casing. Steamed, the fat sausages were the best *boudin noir* I have ever had.

Gumi's pig-slaughter festival ended with a huge porky feast at dinnertime. More relatives and friends came around for the spread. The taste of the meat from the homegrown pigs fed on a diet of grain, corn and leftovers with no other additives was as good as any organic pork money could buy in Beijing. I left the dinner in a pork stupor, glad that I have found another community which enjoyed pork as much as the Chinese, who after all are the biggest consumers of pork in the world.

In the meat-based diet of the Mosuos, there is one treat that is considered by far the best, to be savoured only on special occasions. The treasure is called *zhubiaorou*, a kind of pork fat preserved inside an entire pig. It is the *lardo* of a whole pig carcass with only its fat still attached to its skin, stretched out to retain the shape of a flattened pig.

I first came across *zhubiaorou* when I attended the coming-of-age ceremony of Xiao Wujing. Sitting down to a sumptuous feast laid out with more than a dozen dishes, I saw the host carving slices of pure white *lardo* from a *zhubiaorou* the size of a huge pig. When a plateful was placed before us, the locals zoomed in, ignoring the other goodies on the table. It was obviously their favourite dish.

'In the old days, a family's wealth was measured by the number of *zhubiaorou* kept in the house,' the Mosuo woman next to me said. 'The host will give us a large piece each as a present when we leave. The larger the piece, the more well off is the family.'

To create *zhubiaorou* calls for the skills of a master, and I told Gumi I wanted to start my culinary education.

'My brother is very good at making it. I will add one more pig to the kill and give you your first *zhubiaorou*,' she said.

Starting on pig number two, her brother the butcher master made the first cut from the neck down the middle of the belly to the tail. With consummate care, he opened up the cavity with his hands and removed the entrails. Using short neat cutting strokes, he carefully removed all the meat and bones, all the while making sure he left intact the thick layer of fattish lard lining the skin. He heavily salted the remaining pure fat.

With a big needle threaded with thick twine in hand, he sewed up the entire fatty mass from head to tail, completely sealing the fat within the skin. The entire carcass was patted down and shaped into a flattened pig sculpture. With the utmost care, the men carried the *zhubiaorou* on a piece of cloth to a cool, dry storeroom and left it there to cure and mature over time. The carcass of fat when cured would be protected from the elements by its hardened skin casing. Like cheese and wine, the longer it aged, the better the *lardo* would taste. As tradition dictates, my first *zhubiaorou* now sits in my grandmother's room.

Hunting and gathering remain very much a part of Mosuo living, supplementing the domesticated animals reared at home and the crops grown on the farm. Hunting for meat or gathering edible plant life, which they have done over the ages, is one tradition that is still being passed down from one generation to the next.

At the onset of winter, I always look out for the first flock of Siberian wild ducks to return to Moon Lake. They come by the thousands to nest and roost for the winter, leaving in March when the weather warms up. I never knew that the three varieties of duck that winter here are a source of food for the locals until one morning when Man Friday Jizuo on the horse farm knocked on my door. He held his grandson in one hand and handed me a grey wild duck with the other.

'How did you catch this one?' I asked.

'I put a few traps in the shallow waters of the lake. This one caught its leg on a trap. Here is your dinner,' he said.

What I did not realize at the time when I tasted the most delicious duck soup was that it had become illegal for people to hunt wild things that are designated as protected species under the law. The forestry police are vigilant in enforcing its wildlife protection policy in the Lugu Lake area. While driving deep into the mountains with friends one day, we were stopped at a roadblock and had the boot checked for any signs of a protected animal.

'Someone got caught and fined for killing a wild duck yesterday,' Jizuo said a few weeks later. 'I am going to stop trapping them.'

I told Jizuo about my frequent sightings of an elusive brace of pheasants cavorting about in the small pine forest by Moon Lake. That piqued his interest.

'I used to hunt pheasants with the help of a dog trained to chase them down,' he said, but added after some hesitation, 'they may be protected too, so let's forget it.'

Meat is essential to the local diet, so the Mosuos believe. If possible they would have meat on the table every day. Jizuo explained it this way:

'We need meat to keep us warm in the winter. People like us who live in the high mountains must have meat, otherwise we cannot take the cold.'

This is a widespread notion held by other highland tribes such as the Tibetans. Even Buddhist lamas eat meat-based meals, deviating from the practice observed by Buddhist monks and nuns in China and elsewhere in Asia in following a strictly vegetarian diet. Survival in the harsh mountainous regions may have trumped the need to adhere to an austere regime.

Driven by circumstances in their environment, the Mosuos are imaginative in their search for animal protein in the high mountains. I have come across amazing offerings of wild food by my friends, like the time two friends suggested we went on a frog hunt in my immediate neighbourhood.

The long, wet summer months by Moon Lake spawn a rich season of frogs. I know this by the loud croaking symphony that keeps me awake at night. Our goal that night was to find our own source of frogs' legs. Setting out with a torch each and a plastic bag in hand, we waded gingerly in the shallow waters by the edge of the lake. A small pair of eyes lit up when the light of the torch hit its mark. Momentarily stunned, the frog stood paralysed. The quicker of my two friends swooped down and grabbed it with his hand.

'Open your bag,' he whispered, then placed it inside. By the end of an hour I was holding a bag full of jumping frogs. We returned to the horse farm with our midnight snack of the Mosuo version of this French delicacy.

Animal protein may come in many different and unexpected forms if we open our minds to the possibilities. My Mosuo friends do this with alacrity. One fine afternoon a group of men returned from smoking out a beehive somewhere in the hills on an outing which not surprisingly excluded the women. They showed off their find to the waiting women, a load of beehive combs laden with sticky wild honey. We were happy to divide the spoils among ourselves.

Standing beside me, Zhaxi's *axia*, Erchima, took another look at the remaining combs and smiled broadly.

'Wait,' she exclaimed, 'there is a lot of bee larvae here!'

Taking up a honeycomb, Erchima reached for a single chopstick and dug right into the tiny cell compartments of the comb, dislodging a larvae here or a somnambulant baby gnat there. She gathered a large pile of creepy crawlies in just a few minutes. Popping one in her mouth, she gave me a white bee larva.

'Try this. It's nice.'

I did, with a little hesitancy and my eyes closed. To my amazement, it tasted good, not unlike eating a dried shrimp. I took a second one.

Erchima made her way to my kitchen with the larvae and gnats and heated up the wok with some oil and yak butter. She put the lot into the sizzling oil, added a little salt and Sichuan pepper and with a quick swish turned out the resulting crispy insect fries on a plate. Everyone, including me, tucked in with our chopsticks without any ceremony. The Mosuo treat was devoured within minutes. Enjoying that incredibly strange meal must rate as the most memorable eating experience of my life.

Finding enough wild game and fowl as a regular source of meat has proved increasingly difficult in modern times, with a growing population encroaching upon the habitat of animals in the forest lands. More and more, the Mosuos hunt for fun and pleasure, relying instead on domesticated animals in the farmstead for a steady supply of meat.

The pig, as we have seen, is an important source of meat for them, although it is spaced out sparingly through the year. A Mosuo farm for the most part has no more than a couple of sows and their piglets. The most common meat on the table is a local chicken bred naturally on the farm, again no more than a small number of hens and their chicks. It is not unusual for a farm to add a few ducks and geese.

All the farm animals are let out to roam free in the farmland, feeding on worms and other bits they can find in the field. Back in their pens or coops, the animals are fed with homegrown corn and potatoes topped up with leftover cooked rice and bran. The Mosuos pride themselves in keeping their farm animals additive and chemical free. After all, meat is bred only for home consumption and they mean to feed their family well. There is no incentive for these non-commercial farmers to grow or feed their animals artificially.

Agricultural and veterinary science and technology have made inroads into Mosuo villages, introducing advanced techniques to help improve the farmer's lot and promoting the latest chemicals and feeds. Although typical Mosuo farmers have a cursory knowledge of how these things work, they thumb their noses at incorporating such modern practices into their everyday lives. This is another point of departure from farmers in the more developed farmland elsewhere in China.

Rearing chickens the old-fashioned way takes much longer than keeping them cooped up in cages and injected with growth hormones. A chicken does not end up as dinner in a Mosuo home until it has grown at least five to six months, if not more. A pig is not slaughtered until it has two or three years behind it.

Happily for me, the chicken and duck eggs given by my Mosuo friends come as natural and farm-fresh as they possibly can be, providing me with endless pleasure at the breakfast table. It is hard for me to go back to battery eggs when I return to city living.

Another animal that lives well in the Lugu Lake highlands is the goat. Both species of mountain goat and sheep bred for meat thrive on the grass in the valley. These animals are herded to be sold to locals for special occasions, for lamb or goat is not consumed as an everyday meat. It is not possible to go to the local market to buy a cut of lamb – one has to buy the whole animal directly from a herder.

I once bought a sheep as a culinary treat for my foodie brother on a visit from California. Lee was keen to watch the process of it being cut up from start to finish and I indulged him. I asked the caretaker at the horse farm to act as butcher for the day. He took a mere five minutes to finish the kill and de-skinning. We had a lamb feast that night, with plenty of leftovers.

Carrying on an age-old custom, the Mosuos gather wild plants as another source of food in their Spartan way of life. Springtime in Lugu

Lake brings with it an abundance of wild flowers and other flora all over the countryside. The seasonal change awakens the gatherer in the heart of a Mosuo. Edible greens, berries and fruit, even mountain herbs and roots, are there for the picking.

Trekking in the woods with my godchildren, I watched in amazement as they came across wild strawberries hidden among the vines by the side of the forest path. Nongbu picked a handful of small red ones for me. They were packed with an unexpectedly concentrated strawberry flavour.

When we returned to their home, Gumi met us with a basketful of other wild plants she had gathered on her own foraging ramble.

'What did you find?' I asked.

'Here are leaves I picked from a medicinal plant that can cure colds,' she said, showing me a large bunch. 'These roots I dug up are used in soups. They are good to build up strength.'

Gumi's finds are just two of the hundreds of varieties of medicinal wild herbs, leaves, fruits and roots found in Yunnan and used all over China. The people in this huge country have an undying faith in the efficacy of wild plants and animals based on an unbroken system of traditional Chinese medicine. What started out as traditional folk medicine thousands of years ago has evolved through research and development into a health and lifestyle behemoth involving medical practitioners and a huge industrial pharmaceutical complex. The complex depends on Yunnan to provide one-third of its medicinal herb supply.

But in Gumi's far corner of Yunnan, the Mosuos are reluctant newcomers to this trade, content to gather medicinal plants for their own home use. Only a few of them are enterprising enough to collect or grow such traditional products on a commercial scale.

As summer rolls on, the pine-studded hillocks are bathed in intense sunlight and awash with heavy summer rains. These conditions are the perfect environment for the germination of wild mushrooms all over the forest floor, turning mushroom hunting into a favourite sport at this time of the year.

Everyone I know goes looking for one kind or another of the more than 30 varieties of edible mushrooms in these Yunnan hills. I asked to join the goatherd working on the horse farm on a morning hunt for mushrooms. We walked no more than 300 steps before we came upon a large patch of fungi. I reached out to pick one.

'No, not that one. It's poisonous,' he said loudly.

I was in good hands as we continued to fill two bags full of different types of mushroom.

The most precious wild fungus that can be found in these forests is the pine mushroom, *sung rong* in Chinese. To the locals, the porcini-shaped *sung rong* is renowned for its strong earthy fragrance and rich taste and texture. As its name suggests, it grows around the base of pine trees and is plentiful in pine-studded Lugu Lake. Its summer growing season is short but sweet, and, like the locals, I have my fill of them, bought by the kilo from mushroom pickers hawking their wares at the local market.

Although relatively expensive compared to the more common varieties, *sung rong* fetches stratospheric prices across the Sea of Japan in Tokyo. To the sophisticated Japanese fungi eaters, this mushroom, known to them as the *matsutake*, is the aristocrat of all mushrooms. Their discovery of this highly prized delicacy has made its hunt into a serious commercial activity in Lugu Lake.

Owing to their brief shelf life, *matsutake* mushrooms harvested at early dawn in my neck of the woods must reach Tsukiji Market in Tokyo the next day, ready to be sold at prices in multiples of the price I pay for them locally.

Very much like the illusive hunt for truffles in the Italian country-side, hunting for *sung rong* in the pine forests is a furtive enterprise. Taking to the hills early each morning, the local 'professional' hunters spend the whole day hunting, taking care no one is tracking them to their secret spots. They return to the same hidden locations every year to ensure a constant supply of *matsutake* to be sent to the highest bidders in the lucrative mushroom trade.

'Can you take me along on your *sung rong* hunt?' I have asked many a time when I came across someone involved in the trade.

'Sure, any time,' would come the usual polite reply. But when pressed by me for a time and place to meet, the mushroom hunter would mysteriously say he would call me later. I never did receive any such callback.

The Mosuos grow what they cannot find in the wilderness. Nowadays, rice, corn and potatoes are the staple crops grown around Lugu Lake. Before the idea of rice took root about 40 years ago, the Mosuos grew millet, highland barley, corn and potatoes. In those days they subsisted on a mixture of ground millet and barley as the breakfast cereal and ground-corn grits for lunch and dinner. The grains were ground on giant stones turned by hand or a rudimentary watermill, but these have been replaced by motorized machines.

'I still remember the days when my grandmother made us a very thin gruel with the corn. We were so poor that we never had enough corn to feed the whole family,' Erchima said as she recounted her child-hood days to me.

This conversation took place when she enlisted me to help out with a potato harvest at the horse farm. Here I was, someone who had never seen a potato plant in her life, joining in what turned out to be the best workout on a hot afternoon. I gave myself the simpler job of dropping the spuds into baskets while Erchima's all-woman work team dug and piled them up.

Two of them began the task of digging and dislodging the potatoes from the soil. Wielding a heavy Chinese grub hoe to get the job going, each of them swung the four-foot-long hoe upwards, then down into the hard ground, using gravity to force it deeper, ending with pulling out the soil towards her with the iron blade edge of the hoe, exposing the potatoes. It was backbreaking work but the pair laboured tirelessly across the swathe of the potato field all through the afternoon. The remaining women bent down to pick the potatoes, racing along to keep up with the diggers. Trailing behind them with the easiest chore, I could hardly keep up with the pace of these super-strong women.

The highlight of the harvest season for me is getting a call from Gumi with this cheerful message.

'It's rice harvest time!'

Each time I arrived at Gumi's farm for this big event, her work crew would have turned up ahead of me, eager to get the day started. These farm girls never seemed to shirk from hard work, especially as everything was to be done by hand.

Organizing themselves in groups of three, the first group began cutting, gathering and bundling the long rice stalks. Each person in the next group in the chain took hold of a big bundle and beat the lot against a tarpaulin sheet on the ground in order to dislodge the rice grains. When enough rice was collected, those in the third group picked up a handmade wooden tool to begin threshing the grains free of chaff.

The simple implement is the original version of the Chinese Kung Fu weapon called a *nunchaku*, made famous by the legendary master Bruce Lee in his movies in the 1970s. This Chinese farm tool used to harvest rice was invented hundreds, if not thousands, of years ago, and it defies belief that it is still in use in Lugu Lake.

The Mosuo model is made of three wooden sticks linked together with twine to create a long three-sectional swing stick. I watched one of the women pick up the first segment of the rice tool and in one smooth swing throw the linked wooden arms backwards before bringing it back forward to hit the rice grains with the last stick in a resounding thud. This show of workmanlike grace was a real throwback to a bygone era.

Modern times are coming to Lugu Lake to bring it in line with contemporary agricultural practices in the rest of the country. An electric milling machine has been installed in the village of Baju to replace the ancient threshing tool. The villagers are looking forward to renting an automated rice harvester rumoured to have been bought recently by an enterprising local.

For being part of the family, I would receive from Gumi each year two large bags of rice grown on her farm. It will not do for me to decline the heartfelt gift of her sweat and tears, even if the amount is way too much for the appetite of one. I usually cart away the main bulk of it back to Singapore and Beijing to share with my friends.

The rice harvest season coincides with the appearance of ripening fruit in the village. In every Mosuo backyard, apples, peaches and pears are ready for the picking. It is also the time to collect walnuts, a mainstay of Mosuo snacks as well as a present to be gifted to friends and relatives.

However much the times change, I am sure Mosuo families will keep their ancient custom of honouring the food they gather, hunt or grow through a short but sweet ceremony of first offering it to the *chuo-duo*, the stone altar built at the head of the hearth in front of the Fire God. The grandmother of the house will take the choicest bit of the main meal, usually the chicken head, and place it in a bowl on top of the *chuoduo* as an offering to her maternal ancestors, before murmuring the Mosuo version of grace.

'Let the horsemen have a safe trip. While they are on the road, let them not step on thorns or cross a snake's path. Protect our family. Let peace prevail. Let our family be strong generation after generation. Let the arrows we shoot in our lives find their targets.'

7

How the Mosuo Women Rock

A Mosuo female has many sides to her, and in the years I have lived among her sisterhood I have come to appreciate her multi-faceted make-up and the contributions her confident bearing can give to understanding the heart of a woman and womanhood in general.

My first impression of the Mosuo woman was muted, in the sense that I did not form much of a notion. Typically a Mosuo woman is not particularly statuesque, not much taller than my 5ft 4in frame. I would describe her face as more handsome than beautiful. Sloe-eyed with a slight snub nose, she has an easy smile, revealing strong white teeth. She has a latte-coloured sun-drenched complexion and her face is framed by long, jet-black hair tied back in a loose bun.

She is not one to flaunt her physicality. Plainly dressed, she is unadorned, except for a bracelet and sometimes a simple necklace holding an amulet. Unlike women in other cultures who prettify themselves in competition with other females, she eschews decoration herself. She wears no make-up, not wanting to draw too much attention to her looks.

When I took my first stroll by the jetty in Lige, I offered a tube of lipstick to a Mosuo woman sitting by her pig-trough-shaped boat, waiting to take tourists on a tour round the lake. She smiled but demurred.

'No thank you,' she said, embarrassed, 'I am too shy to use such a strong red colour.'

What a contrast her reaction was compared to the reception I got when I distributed a box of lipstick to the Chinese women in my grandfather's village. Every one of them stretched out her hand to snap up the gift. It is no fast and easy task to get to know a Mosuo woman. She is trained from an early age to be modest, and, coming from a culture of shyness as some sociologists have claimed, appears reserved and takes her time to strike up a friendship with an outsider.

But as she moves back among her own people, she wears a totally different face. The Mosuo woman positively rocks with confidence. It is not an aggressive confidence but a self-assurance that comes from deep within. I see it in her tall and straight-backed gait, and I see it in her easy grace when she glides into her native bonfire dance circle. She even sits tall, never slouching but holding tautly her upper body. Rarely do I see a flabby woman, as almost every one of them is lean and upright, pointing to a life used to toiling on the farm.

My friend the Aha grandmother was elated when I said I would take her to the hot springs a long way from her home. Like her fellow villagers, it was a special occasion for her to go to *the* meeting place where in the old days young women and men congregated for frolic and fun. When we stripped down and got into the hot waters, I could not help but marvel at the sight of this granny Amazon. At 66 and in her birthday suit, Aha grandmother was lean and toned, carrying an enviable six-pack.

Strong in both body and spirit is another way I would describe the Mosuo woman. Gumi is a prime example. My adoptive Mosuo sister thinks nothing of hauling a 30-kilo bag of rice. That is 66 pounds of mass on her back. No manual task is too strenuous and no farm management burden too demanding for this hardy sister of mine.

Erchima is another strong-spirited woman. When Zhaxi, her long-term *axia*, came up with the idea of building the first guesthouse in Lige, it was Erchima who let him construct it on her land and name it after himself. While Zhaxi was the public face in developing Zhaxi Guesthouse from a modest seven-room inn to a 20-room hotel with a barbeque restaurant, Erchima was the one single-handedly managing the fitting out of the rooms, arranging the purchasing of food, working as the chef in the commercial kitchen and taking care of the finances of the business.

Xiao Wujing, the younger of the two children of Erchima and Zhaxi, takes after her mother. By the time I attended Wujing's coming-of-age ceremony, she was already in a provincial school for athletes training as a competitive swimmer. Two years before that, the determined 11-year-old had dreamt of becoming a swimmer. Showing an independence of spirit way beyond her tender age, Wujing badgered her parents to send her there.

After she attained the status of a Grade 1 Provincial Swimmer for Yunnan, I turned up at the Water Cube in Beijing's Olympic Village to see her compete at a national swimming event.

'Wu-Jing! Wu-Jing!' I shouted as she competed in her speciality stroke, the butterfly. The story of how this Little Five-Pounder made her dream come true is a study in true female grit and the support the Mosuos give to their women.

It is natural for a Mosuo girl like Wujing growing up in the rarefied world where the grandmother rules the roost to mature into a self-assured and confident person. Almost every Mosuo woman exudes a natural aplomb that many women elsewhere in the world can only pretend to possess.

Taking the lead is the most natural thing for the self-confident Mosuo female. In their exalted position in this society, women follow some interesting and different etiquette rules in their daily lives. They exhibit a bravura I seldom encounter among women in Chinese society or indeed, Western societies.

At one of our female nights out in a local bar, I saw Gumi's older sister striding up confidently to a table of Mosuo men to greet and offer them a few bottles of beer. She was the first to go round to the men, not the other way round, as I would have expected elsewhere in China.

'*Ri-cher*,' she said in her booming voice, cheering them on in the Mosuo greeting to 'bottoms-up' their beer. She was no shrinking violet. Sitting down with the men, she set the tone for the evening by her infectious laughter and jesting flirtation.

Not only does the natural assertiveness of the Mosuo woman show up within the Mosuo community; the remarkable thing is that her well-spring of self-confidence serves her equally well when she ventures into the outside world.

On my many trips with Erchima to cities like Lijiang or Kunming, I was always amazed to see how competently and comfortably she navigated unfamiliar places and situations, especially taking into account the fact that she was illiterate and could not read a single word on the menu or the directional signs on the road. A bystander would have had no idea of her handicap when she ordered food off the menu or negotiated a bargain in a fancy boutique.

When I accompanied Duojie lama's older sister to a grand society wedding in Kunming, where the guest list included prominent businessmen, politicians and luminaries, it was astounding to watch her holding her own at the dinner table. Not for one moment did this illiterate woman from the countryside show any sign of diffidence or timidity. She was confidence personified.

Growing up in a home and society whose central reference point is the grandmother as the head of a matrilineal household must make a woman feel special, especially as she learns very early on that every family member, female and male, defers to her grandmother. Growing up, she will understand the full import of what that means, that inside every Mosuo home beats a woman's heart.

At the very least she must feel much more special than the Chinese woman who is made to take a back seat in a patriarchal household, where tradition requires her to defer first to her father, then to her husband and, finally, to her son in her old age. Everything connected to the female is relegated to a lesser position. For the Mosuo woman, she is already clothed with privilege from the day she is born because a baby girl born to a Mosuo family is a celebration, not a tragedy as it has always been viewed in the old Chinese culture.

One facet of the Mosuo woman that always brings a smile to my face is her fun-loving nature. Every Mosuo loves a party. Sometimes I think the Mosuo woman parties even harder and more frequently than the man. The women do not do a small lunch party, a genteel tea party or a quiet dinner party. When they party, they eat, drink, sing and dance, and invariably make it a day-into-night affair. They rock like there is no tomorrow.

I learnt this the hard way the first time I hosted a party for my Mosuo friends to mark the blessing of my new home. My invitation to about 20 friends was for lunch. Naturally I planned to cater for a midday meal to fit the size of the crowd.

When I extended my invitation to Gumi, I had told her to bring her family along. What I meant was her *axia*, Gizi, her mother and my two godchildren. What she understood was something quite different. She passed my invitation to her entire matrilineal family. That meant her seven siblings, some maternal cousins, their children and grandchildren, plus assorted friends and neighbours.

They turned up in full contingent, all 40 of them. Following the Mosuo way, an invitation such as mine is treated as an open offer. Over time, I too came to be included as an uninvited guest to many Mosuo *soirées*. Following another tradition, my new guests came bearing gifts of rice, salted meat, yak butter, tea, eggs, a few live chickens and a freshly slaughtered suckling pig.

In a panic, I asked Erchima if she could help to prepare a much bigger feast than the one I had originally planned.

'No problem,' she said, immediately issuing instructions to the womenfolk to start cooking while she herself added some of my new gifts to the pot. Under her capable charge, Erchima rustled up a feast of chicken, pork and lamb dishes for lunch.

The beer and the local moonshine flowed as a volunteer group of helpers served lunch to the guests seated at three small, low tables. Just as swiftly, the first group of diners stood up in order for the tables to be cleared before the next lot took their places.

Lunch being over, I expected the guests to leave. They hung around. They continued to drink. They chatted, and they stayed on.

When the evening sun began to set, Erchima nudged me, saying it was time to serve dinner. The party had suddenly turned into a lunch-cum-dinner event. We managed somehow, but the party did not end. My guests began their serious tippling and stayed till midnight before the party broke up. It was the longest party I had ever hosted.

But my true baptism of fire in partying with Mosuo women came later when Erchima proposed a party on International Women's Day, long declared a public holiday for all women in China.

'This is for us, the women of Lugu Lake. Let's have a party,' she said.

Bright and early on the morning, Erchima arrived at my door with a group of four girlfriends, jokingly introducing them as the directors of the local drinking company. Two token male friends tagged along, doubling up as drivers for the day. They carried cases of beer and Chinese white wine to my grandmother's room.

The drinking began there and then, right through the morning, until the drivers made lunch for us. We resumed our drinking through the afternoon before taking off to town for dinner.

'It is time to visit a bar!' one of the younger women said right after dinner.

Off we trooped to the 'poshest' nightclub in town, which by this time was packed with other women also celebrating International Women's Day. Our party immediately took to the dance floor and sang and danced and drank the night away. That 16-hour drinking marathon was the longest party I have ever attended in my life.

Not only do the Mosuo women party long and hard; I was also to discover that they like their female company very much. A night out for the girls is the way to party. To spice up the all-female outings, the partygoers would invite some fun-loving male friends along to provide the entertainment. What is really different about this is that the women would seldom, if ever, take their own *axias* along.

I never figured out the reason for this. Perhaps the women never feel incomplete without their *axias* by their side. Perhaps having their *axias* along would cramp their style. Perhaps the women would rather take the opportunity to play the field. Whatever the reason, I know there is a lesson somewhere here for me.

Another facet of the Mosuo woman is her endearing sense of humour. On seeing the funny side of things, she does not hesitate to be the first to crack a joke, often beating the men to it. In fact, I find the Mosuos, both women and men, love to have a good laugh, any time, anywhere. It is just that the self-confident Mosuo woman feels as much entitled to be the humorist as her male counterpart.

I know very well at first hand how difficult it is for most women in a male-dominated corporate environment to find a humorous voice. In my previous corporate life, I had attended too many business meetings where it was invariably the ultra-confident alpha male who dominated the meeting and cracked the jokes. It took me years to learn that he, or she for that matter, who made the meeting laugh carried the day.

Well, here in the Kingdom of Women it is often the Mosuo woman who takes centre stage and plays the consummate standup comic, if she so desires. In fact, both women and men often resort to humour when they get together, which makes it really fun to hang out with them. What impresses me is that in mixed company, the women are just as likely as the men to be the ones with the jokes. That to me speaks volumes about the place women hold in their society.

Back at home, a Mosuo woman gives as good as she takes. She does not shy away from giving her opinion if she has one. Her voice carries weight within the home, with grandmother's voice carrying the final veto.

I once overheard Erchima and her maternal family discussing an important issue relating to the division of family land, including the plot on which Zhaxi Guesthouse sat. The discussion grew more and more heated, until someone bought this up:

'What does Zhaxi say about this?'

'He has no say in this matter. He is not family,' Erchima retorted, even though Zhaxi was her long-term *axia*.

Yet, matriarchy notwithstanding, Mosuo women have fashioned a world based more on equality between the genders than the superior-inferior model adopted by traditional Chinese culture. In their social interactions, I see many instances of a power structure that is more balanced than in a patriarchal setting.

Everyone, it appears, is treated more or less equally – women to men, women to women, men to women, men to men, old to young. I had often watched as the grandmother in Jizuo's home started a conversation with her grandchildren in grown-up speak, not baby talk, and patiently waited for their talkback. In more instances than I can count, I had assumed someone having a casual conversation with Zhaxi was a friend or business associate of his by the respectful and even-handed way he treated that someone. It would turn out that the person was Zhaxi's employee. This is in strict contrast to a Chinese boss, who would make it plain by his speech and manner that he was talking down to an employee.

The women would sometimes resort to using the occasional diminutive barb demeaning men or male behaviour, and there are many of these in the Mosuo language, but this is never elevated to an institutionalized, fossilized system of unequal treatment of men. I sense the Mosuos live with a different and more equal value system when it comes to women–men relations, in direct contrast to the Chinese preference for talking down to women.

Going back to basics, a key facet of a Mosuo woman's existence is her natural ability to become a mother and thereby add to the matrilineal headcount at home. To be a first-time mother is the greatest celebration in a Mosuo woman's life. It is a time for congratulations from relatives and friends. Conversely, a woman who has never given birth is to be pitied.

A Mosuo mother is proud to play mother, and she will carry her baby tied with a cloth on her back everywhere in the old-fashioned way. That is how Ercher shows off my new goddaughter in Lige. When it is feeding time, Ercher, like all the new mothers I know in Lugu Lake, does the most natural thing in full public view. Untying her portable

111

baby carrier, she cradles the little girl in her arms, flips up her blouse and starts breastfeeding, now and then switching from one nipple to the other. Nobody looks, nobody flinches. If Ercher had done this in public in, say, Shanghai or Beijing, she would have been the object of ridicule and condemnation, with a video of her breastfeeding going viral on all the internet chat groups.

The one distinctive characteristic of a Mosuo mother is that traditionally she is eternally a 'single' mother from the perspective of outsiders. Any child she bears is necessarily born out of wedlock because she is not married and does not have a man claiming ownership over her child. Strictly in Chinese patriarchal terms, she commits a scandalous act each time she gives birth to a child and continues to bring dishonour to her family by remaining a single mother.

But none of these outrageous condemnations will ever surface in a community that celebrates motherhood within the confines of a purely matrilineal family structure. A Mosuo baby is necessarily born of a mother outside the inconceivable idea of marriage, and is by definition father-less in a society that pays no heed to fatherhood.

By far the most interesting facet of the Mosuo woman and one that has attracted the most attention in China and around the world is her *axia* lifestyle. In fact it is much more than a lifestyle choice that the Mosuo woman, like the Mosuo man, is fundamentally free in her society to choose an *axia*, or any number of them, through the course of her life. She does this in a community that is free from the necessity of marriage between a woman and a man to form a nuclear family. She does this in the comfort and privacy of her maternal home. Furthermore she is free to close the door in her flower chamber to a temporary lover and open it to the next. This must count as the most revolutionary side to her life, at least to all of us outside the Mosuo world where marriage is the starting point of family life.

In this space of infinite possibilities, it is logical to assume that the criteria used by a Mosuo woman in choosing a male *axia* will be radically different from those that apply in choosing a permanent partner for marriage. For such a woman, an *axia* is a delightful digression from the drudgery of everyday life as well as a potential sperm donor. The criteria then should be fit for its purpose.

The Mosuos have figured out a long time ago that a woman's seed can only become green grass growing on the ground if the seed is watered by rain from the sky, as my friend the eminent Chinese social anthropologist Cai Hua explained in his seminal work on the Mosuo *axia* system, *A Society without Fathers or Husbands*. A woman bearing the seed of childbirth needs a man to water it to bring forth life.

It therefore goes without saying that the water of life must be precious enough in the looks department to enable the seed to grow big, strong and beautiful. From the perspective of a woman wanting a baby, the man who provides the water must first and foremost be good looking and well built.

In looking for a mate, and here I use the word 'mate' in its primary procreative sense, the Mosuo woman seeks out what to her are the attractive physical attributes in a man. High up on the list are brawn and beauty. It cannot get more frank and direct than that.

On seeing a water bearer, the questions racing in a woman's mind are likely to be the following:

'Is he tall and robust?'

'Is he handsome?'

'Does he have big strong hands?'

'Is he sturdy enough to manage heavy manual work?'

Time and again on our girls' nights out, I have been privy to more bawdy jokes about men and their ranking on the desirability scale than I can recall.

'How about this one?' someone would typically ask the group when a man passed by but not within earshot.

'Not handsome enough,' one of us would respond, to guffaws all around.

'That one looks delicious,' a young woman friend exclaimed one night on seeing a dashing good looker moving on the dance floor.

And so it goes on.

Because of the unique circumstances of the Mosuo matrilineal family make-up where the 'waterer' is not a member of the household and therefore not a contributor to its wellbeing, a Mosuo woman is not bothered about the size of his wallet. A Beijing fat cat would not necessarily fit the bill. Whether he has a fast car, a huge mansion or acres of farmland does not matter to the woman in her overall scheme of things. It is irrelevant whether or not he is the responsible type. After all, she will never set up home with him nor will she depend on him for her or her family's survival. He just needs to have good-quality water to do the job.

Besides having eye-candy appeal, a man can do well if he is amusing and has a good sense of humour, if only to make time spent with him more pleasurable. Not forgetting that love, when it happens for a Mosuo woman, can be a fleeting occurrence. Not so strange after all, even for the rest of us, if only we would stop and think about it.

A Mosuo woman is not shy in expressing her desire for the man of the moment. There are no dating rules requiring her to be coy or to hold back. There is no shame about being brazenly forward. Because she is free from any such social opprobrium, she will let her heart speak directly through the uninhibited gaze of her eyes on her object(s) of desire.

In a moment of reflection on her love life, a Mosuo woman may find her own image floating on the surface of Lugu Lake. There, lavishly strewn all over the blue water, are tiny waterweed flowers with their pretty white heads moving gracefully with the flowing tide, as if beckoning onlookers to come closer. Hidden underwater are their long roots trailing all the way to the bottom of the inland sea. The Chinese have a phrase for these florets, *shuixing yanghua*, loaded with a poetic *double entrendre*. Literally it means flowers waving in the water, and, figuratively, it refers to a woman of easy virtue.

No doubt a sceptic from the male-dominant Chinese culture would see a Mosuo woman coming across as promiscuous. In her own culture, the prettiest girl, like the *shuixing yanghua*, would never be chastised for being promiscuous. Instead she would be applauded for attracting a bevy of *axias*.

If the analogy of the floating blossom is too simplistic, the Mosuo woman need only cast her eye towards her protectrix deity reclining astride the grand lake for a more inspiring resemblance. After all, the imposing Gemu Mountain Goddess is indisputably the quintessential Mosuo woman who rocks.

Gemu is like no other deity I know. Unlike the self-righteous, sanctimonious, monotheistic male gods strutting their stuff around the world, this divine guardian spirit of the Mosuo people has been inspirited by her people with a much more human face. And it is in keeping faith with the goddess's peccadilloes that the Mosuos have kept alive their unique perspectives on life and love.

According to folklore, Gemu began her life as a mortal. But she was no mere earthling. Blessed with an extraordinary intelligence, she was wise beyond her years. Moreover she was so unbelievably beautiful that all the men and even the gods and demons in the universe were smitten with her. She paid a dear price for being such a ravishing madonna.

While she was singing by Lugu Lake one day, a demon god spirited her away and kept her all to himself in the heavens above. Being deprived of her lovely company, the Mosuos grieved and cried so hard and loud that their pleas for her return were heard by the highest celestial being. He ordered her to be released back to her people. There was a slight hitch, however. He sent Gemu back not as a mortal but in the form of a grand mountain and ordered her to be the guardian deity of the Mosuos.

Back in the cradle of her Mother Lake, Gemu settled down to her role as carer for and custodian of her matrilineal community. Her day job in these peaceful and idyllic lands left her free to pursue her leisure in the evenings and on off days. In adoration, the becharmed Mosuos painted her as a dutiful guardian with a fun-loving nature. Their portrait of her is as a beautiful woman sitting resplendently on a white horse with a twinkle in her eye revealing a playful character full of hedonistic tendencies. She likes to have fun, enjoys a good party, imbibes alcohol like a man and loves to gamble and throw a dice or two.

And true to their unique perspective on their love life, their Goddess is imbued with a spirited enjoyment of her men friends. Not one to lack suitors, Gemu Goddess is reputed to have chosen the tallest, most magnificent male mountain god known as Puna as her main *axia*. Puna became her constant companion, that is, when he is around. But whenever he takes leave to do whatever male mountain gods do while on the road, Gemu does not let the opportunity pass. She seizes the chance to flirt with other mountain gods lurking in the vicinity. A handsome mountain god to the north, Ah Shang, catches her roving eye. There were others for the picking, one mountain to the northwest, and another couple of mountain gods to the south, all of whom have had a dalliance with her as her 'short-term' *axia*. Nothing wrong with that, because all is fair in the Mosuo game of love.

I love the Gemu story, down to her playful ways with the mountain gods. So do the Mosuos, who see Gemu as the inspiration to romance and love, and use it to justify their multi-partner code of love. As an old Mosuo adage goes, if Gemu Mountain Goddess practises it, so will they.

I see a distinct common thread that runs through the diverse facets of a Mosuo woman's life. It is the thread of the empowerment of the female. The quality most valued by a Mosuo mother is a daughter's intelligence, for the little girl will be chosen to take over the reins of running the mother's household when the time comes.

A Mosuo girl is born free from cultural and societal restrictions to party, laugh, lead, toil and love. She has no need to fight for empowerment because she is empowered from birth. She comes from a long line of empowered mothers, grandmothers and beyond, all revered as vital members of the community, headed at the pinnacle by their Mountain Goddess. In a way, she is so used to the idea of an empowered existence that she accepts it all 'as is'. There is no push to wear it on her sleeve or shout it from the mountaintop. There is no war to begin with. From the very start, she is born to this high status. She carries that empowerment throughout her life, cocooned in a world that celebrates the female.

For me, taking a leaf from the Mosuo lasses is like peeking through the other side of the looking glass. They represent a refreshing reversal of roles. The tables are turned the other way around in more ways than one. Small wonder that I feel at one with my Mosuo sisters. Mine is a camaraderie of like-minded, sure-footed women.

Mosuo women will make every true-blooded female like me feel vindicated for appreciating men who are pleasing to her eye, purely for their basic physical attributes. To my mind, there is nothing wrong with this approach. It can be liberating for a woman to break free from looking for other non-relevant, intangible qualities in a male partner, especially if he is to be temporary. And contrary to the common perception in conventional societies that women will make bad choices of men if they opt only for good looks, the Mosuo sisterhood will gladly attest to the times when they let beauty and brawn take precedence over the other things.

I suppose in a very real sense, the unusual multi-faceted Mosuo woman in totality is girl power at its best. I get it. I get it as a woman emboldened by the example set by the confident Mosuo woman. I get it as I think back to myself as a confident five-year-old girl who so believed in myself that I fearlessly took on my brother and the other boys in the neighbourhood in a peeing-against-the-wall contest. I lost that battle but it spurred me on to a lifetime of standing up and fighting for female equality and for the rightful place of women in my world.

I also know full well that my views will not be shared by mainstream Chinese society. A *shuixing yanghua* to a Chinese man will always be promiscuous and that is a bad thing if the woman happens to be his wife or daughter. However, it can be a good thing if he is given the chance to enjoy her promiscuity for a night or two.

I believe that there are many Chinese men who come to Lugu Lake in search of their *shuixing yanghua*, if only just for the few days they stay as tourists. Sometimes they get lucky. At other times the more demanding tourists expect to get lucky and will willingly pay for it. The question is whether the Mosuo woman is willing to go along with the idea that her *axia* love is for sale.

In the early years of the tourist trade, some enterprising operators opened brothels in Luoshui, the first Mosuo lakeside village at the juncture where the highway from Lijiang meets Lugu Lake. There, buses deposited tourists at these 'sex spots' and whisked the men into tiny rooms while keeping the female tourists busy drinking tea and looking at silver trinkets. A woman dressed Mosuo-style would be waiting in each of the rooms to service the men. A Beijing friend of mine told me that she waited a long time before her father surfaced from one of these rooms when her family toured Lugu Lake more than ten years ago. Her father never spoke about what happened in the room.

Prostitution in Luoshui grew so rampant that the villagers had to petition the local authorities to deal with the problem. Their solution was to move all the brothels to a remote corner of Luoshui, which the villagers came to call the red-light district. The brothels are still there.

When I broached the subject with my Mosuo friends, they would invariably respond by saying that the prostitutes working there were real professionals brought over from the neighbouring province of Sichuan, and not Mosuo women plying the trade. This may be true in the majority of the cases, but some Mosuo women are definitely involved.

The good thing that came out of the Luoshui experience is that other tourist hamlets along Lugu Lake have banned sex tourism in their backyards. But there is one more village in the vicinity whose economy is supported by scarf weaving and prostitution, and that is Wenjuan, home to the famous hot springs in the Mosuo hills.

'Almost every other home in Wenjuan has a daughter who is a prostitute,' a friend told me. 'The families are not ashamed of it. In fact, they feel proud that their daughter is earning good money for the family.'

With prostitution, as well as the high incidence of multiple-partner sex among the Mosuos, the spread of sexually transmitted diseases is inevitable. It is fair to say that this is a recurring health problem among both women and men in the Mosuo community, although no one talks about the subject openly.

No one has kept statistics, and modern medical facilities have only become available in Yongning in recent times. A consequence is that some children are born with disabilities. Although not immediately apparent when I look around the community, I have met a young girl who has been blind from birth and a handicapped man with deformed hands and feet. There is a story of a woman in her 40s who developed a mental condition, which eventually pushed her to suicide. Whether STD was the cause is uncertain. Also uncertain is whether STD has affected fertility, but again this is hard to tell because the number of children born to a woman is complicated by China's family-planning policy. Like in the rest of the country, Mosuo women use contraception to control childbirth, limiting themselves to two children per household.

Sex for love or money is a perennial question in all societies and Lugu Lake is no exception. But its existence in the Mosuo community does not detract from the larger universal issues thrown up by the Mosuo model of womanhood in the face of patriarchal society.

The first issue is the very existence of a woman-centric society in a sea of patriarchy that has inundated the whole world. The fact that the Mosuo paradigm exists at all calls into question the inevitability of human society evolving as the male-dominant archetype. The Kingdom of Women has shown that is possible to have an alternative model.

The second issue is forging a better environment in which a woman can be nurtured and fostered to reach her full potential as a complete, confident person ready to contribute as meaningfully as a man to society. The male-centric model of patriarchy is obviously not the solution, looking at how the world treats women today and yesterday. The Mosuo model that puts the female at its centre without downgrading the male to purgatory appears to be a much better option.

The third issue is whether elevating women from their second-class position in society to the prime spot would bring an end to the human race. Of course not, as the Mosuos have shown us.

The final issue is the valuable lesson the Mosuo woman teaches all the single women in Chinese society. They are the 'left behind' women, having failed to find a man to marry, and so piteous that they are ranked last behind all the other women in the social hierarchy of the genders. They can learn to wear their singlehood with pleasure and honour, just as I have done.

In a mad moment when I was particularly happy in my Mosuo home, I had a vision that I must have been a Mosuo woman in a past life. How else could I make sense of the feeling of connectedness I feel in the midst of my Mosuo friends, never again having to fight against overt male chauvinism in my previous law firms in Singapore or be as aggressive as the next man in an all-male network of lawyers in Los Angeles.

Perhaps I could compare my DNA with Gumi's to see if we came from the same original clan mother of our ancient tribes. I swabbed Gumi's inner cheek and sent the specimen to a genetics laboratory in Oxford for testing. Her result confirmed that her direct maternal ancestor is Malaxshimi, whose clan is found today in the southern parts of Asia and on the islands of the Pacific as well as in Mongolia, Korea, India and Pakistan. Quite different from my being a direct maternal descendent of Ina, born in the Cook Islands of Eastern Polynesia and herself the clan mother of four major clans which colonized North and South America from Eastern Asia many millennia ago.

I was disappointed to say the least. Gumi, my Mosuo sister, and I do not share the same clan mother. We are not related in our ancient maternal bloodlines. But in my heart of hearts, I am sure we share a common, glorious female spirit.

8

The Men Rock Too

We now come to the other half of the story in the Kingdom of Women. It is the Adam side of the chronicle in this unique land where most things we hold true are turned upside down, with a community that revolves around women but which values men for their secondary but special place in society.

There is an oft-cited old saying that encapsulates the male core of Chinese society. 'Zhong Nan Jing Nu' is something I can imagine my paternal grandmother would have liked to say to my ten-year-old self whenever I questioned why she favoured my firstborn brother over me. The words literally mean 'Indulge the boys, lighter on the girls', and describe how patriarchal Chinese society almost makes it a religion to treat boys much better than girls. The maxim that the male dominates while the female submits has prevailed in Chinese culture for thousands of years and is still largely the norm today, although it has been somewhat diluted due to the one-child policy prevailing in the Chinese cities.

Borrowing but paraphrasing the dictum, I think the best way to juxtapose the position of girls and boys in Mosuo society is to come up with an alternative saying, 'Zhong Nu Bu Jing Nan'. Read literally this means 'Indulge the girls, (but) not lighter on the boys'.

This coinage of mine is not the direct opposite of the patriarchal saying. It is not 'Indulge the girls, lighter on the boys', because that is not the way the Mosuos think, that women are superior to the men beneath. Unlike the Chinese, the more egalitarian Mosuos, while cherishing girls born to their families because they go on to preserve their matrilineage, do not displace the boys to a lower and lesser position. Boys who grow up to be men are not belittled. Like girls, they too have a place in the sun.

To put this in the right context, it is best to start with a discussion of what places the Mosuo man does not inhabit under the sun. Firstly, a Mosuo man is eternally a 'single' man, just as the Mosuo woman is single. He is not a husband in a marriage-less society. Secondly, he is never a father in the sense that we understand it, precisely because Mosuo society is father-less.

What is left for the Mosuo man is so unlike the experience of the patriarchal man that it takes a big leap of our imagination to follow the storyline. One of the first things an outsider will notice is that the Mosuo man is essentially a mummy's boy.

'I am going back to my mother's to have dinner with her,' are the words frequently spoken by a peripatetic male friend of mine who has made his living as a long-distance tour-bus driver.

'Sorry, but I am taking my mother to the doctor's in Lijiang,' another man said, excusing himself from a dinner at Gumi's house.

The Mosuo man is indeed his mother's boy because he lives his whole life with her in his maternal home. He is a fully fledged member of that matrilineal household that includes all his other siblings born to his mother, as well as his other maternal relatives. To him, his mother, and by extension, his grandmother, are the most important elders in his life.

'I will sing the Mosuo song about love for mother,' is the common refrain I hear when a man is made to choose a track to sing at the many karaoke sessions I have attended with my Mosuo friends. That particular ode to mother love is the big hit among my male friends.

Another place reserved for the Mosuo man is his mentoring role as the uncle to all the children of his sisters. Although he has no fathering duties to any of the children of his *axia*(s), he does carry the weighty responsibility of looking after his maternal nieces and nephews. As an uncle he is the pivotal male influence over the children, much like that of a father in a nuclear family. Part of this role is to pass on the skills needed for survival and the folklore laying down the moral compass for the children.

It is always interesting for me to see this uncle-niece-nephew relationship being played before my eyes. When Zhaxi gets together with his niece and my goddaughter, Ladzu, he makes a special effort to hold her hand and talk at length with her. The same goes for Nongbu in his warm relationship with his maternal uncle who is an elder brother of Gumi.

When a Mosuo man grows older and becomes the oldest male at home, he assumes the elevated position of being the great uncle and the co-head of the matrilineal family by virtue of being the brother of the matriarch of the household. In the Aha household, it is clear to me that the two younger generations of grandmother's children and grandchildren observe a strict formality in paying respect to the brother of grandmother Aha. As the co-head, the great uncle's voice carries almost as much authority as his sister's, particularly as he is the highest-ranking teacher and mentor among the men in the household. His additional role outside the home is to represent the family in community affairs such as village meetings. Altogether he occupies a not inconsequential place in the matrilineal family.

My godson Nongbu has six maternal uncles upon whom he can call for guidance. He has learnt his manners and other social skills from them. More than that, it is also from them that Nongbu has mastered the everyday skills of riding a horse, catapulting at birds and fishing in the streams.

It is evident to me that Nongbu and Ladzu and their cousins have been taught a strict code of conduct to show respect to all those older than them, ranging from their circle of maternal aunts and uncles to the village elders and even an outsider godmother like me. Every Mosuo youngster that I have come across has been a model of respectfulness at a level I seldom see among Chinese children.

Nongbu is a walking embodiment of the gallant and considerate young man, as I found out on my first outing with him. Then only ten years old, he and his sister led me on a mushroom hunt up on a hillock behind their house. With his sister taking the lead, the small boy followed behind, bouncing along ahead of me to show the way as I took up the rear. As he came across a clump of tall bushes blocking the forest trail, he immediately stood aside and held the branches away from the path with his hands.

'I am clearing the way for you,' he announced in his still unbroken voice.

He only let go of the thorny bush after I had walked past it.

As we climbed on he kept a vigilant lookout, occasionally glancing back to make sure I was all right. When we reached a particularly steep slope, he turned around to offer his tiny hand to me, and as I took it he mustered all the strength he had to hoist me up the rise.

I was pleasantly surprised to find such gallantry in so young a boy. His thoughtfulness did not wane as he grew older. Walking next to me, he would never let me carry a load, be it a shopping bag or my large handbag which he cheerfully lugged over his shoulder.

A Mosuo, whether female or male, displays an ingrained gallantry throughout her or his life. I had never needed to carry my own luggage as long as there was a Mosuo man around. If I happened to bump into a Mosuo woman or man I knew while at the market, the friend would invariably offer to carry all my shopping bags.

Every Mosuo man in his adult years knows that his main role at home is to carry out the heavy-duty manual tasks in his grandmother's farmstead. His brawn is his contribution and he is expected to use his muscles in the service of the family.

A full day's work for Jizuo, Gumi's brother, reads like a catalogue of laborious tasks. On any given day, he might start by chopping firewood, followed by rebuilding the mud wall surrounding the house. I witnessed him single-handedly putting up a new extension to the existing barn at home. Often he would be summoned by a relative to haul big boulders by hand to build the stone foundations for a new house. He would be the one pushing the buffalo-led plough across the rice field and carting the large bales of ripened rice stalks home. The heaviest jobs around and outside the house were reserved for him.

Gumi speaks often of her father and the tough times he endured as a stable hand. In his younger days when the larder at home was empty, he would join other men to lead packhorses on arduous treks from Lugu Lake all the way to Tibet. On the outward journey he would have had to pack bales of tea and medicinal herbs on to horses and walk along the ancient tea-horse trail for a couple of months before arriving at his destination. On the return journey he would have had to pack up once more, loading up carpets and other Tibetan handicrafts, to make his way back. In those pre-cash-economy days, he would have been paid in kind, some millet or highland barley or perhaps a goat-skin coat.

Both the two sons of Gumi's eldest brother make their living alternating as drivers of their big lorry. They earn good money from their haulage enterprise, but the service they provide not only entails driving long distances but also getting their hands dirty, lifting and unloading the heavy cargoes they transport.

The Mosuo man gets richly rewarded when he returns home after a hard day's labour. The grandmother makes sure to give him the lion's share of the scarce meat in the pot when she doles out the food to the family that night.

That a Mosuo grandmother would take time to indulge her son or grandson when he has earned it is testimony to her sense of fair treatment between the women and men in her matrilineal family.

This jogs my memory to a surreal scene I witnessed in the home of a girlfriend in Singapore whose family belonged to a particularly paternalistic dialect group of the Teochews from the south of China. To my shock, only the men sat down at the dinner table when the food was laid out. They took their time enjoying their dinner before getting up to make way for us, the women, to pick at the leftovers. This unequal treatment would not have gone down well with the Mosuo grandmother.

In between the heavy jobs, Mosuo men are encouraged to take time out to have fun. In fact they take a lot of time out to do what macho men do when they want to have fun. Their idea of fun is to hang out with the boys to eat, drink, fight while drunk, quite different from the youth in the Chinese cities, and pursue hobbies from the past.

A favourite pastime is hunting. This is a sport meant only for the menfolk, who are understood by the grandmother to be really boys disguised in adult clothing. At the drop of a hat, a Mosuo man will jump up, eyes glinting, gather his hunting tools and run to the hills with his pals.

Zhaxi and his men friends would often use the horse farm as the staging post to go hunting for anything wild, be it honey from bee hives on the trees, fish in the lake, flights of rice birds from the fields, bevies of pheasants in the woods, paddlings of wild ducks on Moon Lake or the occasional wild hog on the run. I would see the cheerful lot of them departing early in the morning and returning at nightfall with a catch or two, or sometimes nothing at all. Yet they seemed pleased to have spent the day doing what their forefathers had done many lifetimes ago.

By far the most fun and pivotal role a man plays in the tableau of Mosuo life is to take the part of the 'stud' in the life cycle of the Mosuo family. His job, as the anthropologist Cai Hua says in his book, is to give rain for the grass to grow on the ground. He is the quintessential water bearer, his task being to nourish the seed in the woman in order for a baby to be made. After all, every woman looks forward to having babies to add to her matrilineal family and she knows she needs the help of the man to 'water the grass'. The man, on the other hand, is only too happy to do the charitable thing, watering to his heart's content.

To this end, a Mosuo man trains and auditions hard for the part. I think he has found the most appropriate role model in the archetypal peacock. A male peacock, in order to catch the attention of his mate, does several essential things. It grows tall and strong and develops a proud gait, preening itself to ensure it is in peak condition for the mating season. Strutting about grandly, it shows off its decorative and larger-than-life tail feathers in search of love.

It always amazes me to see an unusually high concentration of macho men swaggering about like the proverbial peacock when I stroll about the local market. Often a young man catches my eye as he passes by. Sturdily built, he has his long black hair tied up in a fashionable pony-tail, looking positively trendy. Ahead, striding in front of me, will be another tall, rather good-looking fellow gazing at the world from under his jaunty big hat. Another one will strut across my path and I cannot help but take notice of his exaggerated he-man gait.

I think most women who come to Lugu Lake will agree with me when I say that generally Mosuo men are exceedingly big on looks. They are a handsome lot, and in a strange way seem much better looking than their female counterparts. Their attractiveness lies not only in their appearance; it is also their vainglorious narcissistic and self-conscious masculinity that makes up the entire striking package.

Let me try to put these notions down in picture form. Randomly I could pick any of the men I glimpse in the marketplace, and would find a face that is striking with its strong, chiselled features. His blue-black eyes would peer through double eyelids beneath thick expressive eyebrows. He would breathe through an aquiline nose, not too long, not too short, shaped in a 45-degree angle in profile, sharper than the flat, broad nose typical of the majority of men one sees in China. He would smile a mischievous smile. He would wear a heavily tanned face usually topped with a cowboy hat poised purposely at a rakish angle to set off his cheeky eyes.

That handsome face would be all the more stunning on a well-built, brawny frame. A Mosuo man is not usually short, occasionally reaching six feet in height. Physically, he is well built, complete with bulging muscles and a six-pack torso with no need of daily gym workouts. In the hot summer months, many a vain Mosuo man parades about in a sleeveless T-shirt to show off his well-developed biceps.

A Mosuo man has the most massive and manly-looking hands I have ever set eyes on. Not only is his palm span larger than a normal male hand, his fingers are thicker and longer than most. Other men take notice.

'Wow!' said a young and obviously athletic Japanese tourist when he matched his relatively puny hand to Zhaxi's one day at the guesthouse. 'What a he-man!'

Like a consummate actor, a Mosuo man knows that looks can only go so far. Somehow he has figured out that he must also act out the part of the he-man to get the women. He has learnt to let his bearing and body language shout out his masculinity. Very consciously he choreographs his every pose and move to let his macho essence come through.

I am certain that every Mosuo man rehearses his act before stepping out of the door. How else can I explain the commonplace phenomenon of him literally striking an eye-catching pose in public or making a move with a studied manly 'cool' whenever he is in female company. It is obvious that he has honed his craft over the years to bring his peacock act to perfection.

The Mosuo male starts young at peacocking. Jizuo has a grandson called Xiao Liujing, Little Six-Pounder, who at barely five years old is a peacock in waiting.

'Xiao Liujing, sing us a song,' a familiar face shouts out at him as he enters Zhaxi Guesthouse with his grandfather.

Without skipping a beat, the little boy grabs a paper cup and holds it against his mouth like a microphone, strikes up a pose and starts belting out a current hit. As he sings, he punctuates his performance with fancy dance moves, prancing to the beat, hands sweeping wide, hips gyrating, all the time preening himself like a seasoned rock star. He ends with a flourish, closing his eyes in a dramatic finale. He is a veritable pro.

Serenading by song is a well-worn stratagem the Mosuo man uses to gain a woman's attention. In the old days he would have broken out in a full-throated *a capella* directing his love ballad across the lake to the beauty waiting onshore while rowing by in his dinghy. Using the same two-stanza tune, he would improvise the lyrics to the ditty, hoping his wit would elicit a positive response from his object of desire:

Ahabala Madami,
I see a brilliant red flower on the shore,
Can it be a bloom sent from Gemu Mountain Goddess to brighten up
my day?

Because he was able to throw his voice loud and far, his song would
have reached his intended audience of one. Amused, she would play
along in this age-old practice of 'cross-singing', the Mosuo way of flirting. She would be ready to throw back a rejoinder, sung to the same
tune:

Balayaha Aleuleu!
Is that a fat pig I see trying to sing a song?
I didn't know pigs could sing.

'Ah, she is interested,' he thinks. 'Better go along and play the fool':

Ahabala Madami!
Only handsome pigs sing to beautiful flowers.
Although flowers are usually kinder than the voice I hear.

Mosuos do not do much cross-singing anymore as it has fallen out
of fashion. But occasionally I have been privy to humorous romantic
ditties performed as an after-dinner entertainment, enacted in a crowd
of middle-aged Mosuos who can recall the old ways of romance.

The Mosuos set great store on song and dance. Many villages and
hamlets around Lugu Lake hold nightly community dance perfor-
mances to catch the tourist trade. The Mosuo male dancers come into
their own as they take the lead in the *jiachuo* dance. Setting the rhythm
for the dance, they stomp their way around the floor with unapologetic
vigour. As they get into the performance, each male dancer tries to
outdo the next guy, taking a bigger step, kicking his legs higher and

stamping the ground harder. Joining in a chorus at the top of their voices, they bellow out instructions for the next variation in the dance steps. Every move is executed in the name of showmanship. These Mosuo men really rock.

The name of the game for the Mosuo man is to use every opportunity to catch the attention of a woman as a peacock would his potential mate. To this end, each man without exception is a natural-born show-off, and what he means to show is how physically macho and attractive he is to women. Each move he makes, each swagger he exhibits, is exaggerated. He does not simply dance. He *performs* his dance. He does not merely sing a folk song. He performs it like a rock star. He does not just walk. He struts about like Tarzan in the forest. Above all, he preens himself so as to look like a real man in front of the womenfolk. All of which make Mosuo men very attractive to women indeed. It is an attractiveness that is packaged to spell MACHO, in capital letters.

The prime example of the proud peacock is the modern-day Lugu Lake legend widely acknowledged as the 'Mosuo Prince of Walking Marriages'. There are multiple references to this person on Chinese travel websites. The first part of his nickname is no doubt a tribute to this quintessential Mosuo he-man who is reputed to have charmed so many women that it would be pointless to keep count. The second part of his name is a reference to the practice of Mosuo love life not tied to marriage or life-long monogamy, where a man 'walks' to his (current) lover's home to spend the night with her but returns home to his matrilineal homestead the morning after.

The famous, and some say infamous, Don Juan of Don Juans is none other than the uncle of my godchildren and the architect-cum-builder of my house, Zhaxi. This towering six-footer is truly a picture of macho perfection, his fine face, enviable well-built physique and ultra-masculine charisma an immediate draw for anyone meeting him for the first time. He looks like a great Mohawk chief come down from the mountains to conquer everyone in his path. This stunning Mosuo man with a deep gravelly voice to match is a remarkable showman who has single-handedly pushed up tourism figures to Lugu Lake over the last decade. Everyone it seems looks for Zhaxi on arriving in Lige. He has been photographed so many thousands of times by visitors that he has perfected the art of posing and holding his gaze for the camera far more expertly than the Tom Cruises of the world.

I have watched many a woman tourist swoon unabashedly over Zhaxi, who in the land of colourful peacocks, is the megastar. He has legions of women fans who come from near and far just to catch a glimpse of him. And it is not just the women.

Even men find his stud-like qualities attractive. I have seen grown men look on this Romeo par excellence with a mix of undisguised envy and utter admiration when they come face to face with him. Envy, I think, because this Mosuo specimen coming across as undiluted masculinity calls into question the onlooker's own masculinity, and admiration because a man always defers to another male who is bigger and more manly than he is. Zhaxi is so self-confidently macho that the local men around him look to him as the leader of their pack. A Singapore male friend of mine refers to him as 'Rambo'.

I became curious to find out just where Zhaxi's ancestors came from at the same time I was collecting a mouth swab from Gumi to test her lineage. I managed to get Zhaxi to let me swab his inner cheek. His test results came back as a complete surprise. His genes revealed that he was descended from the paternal clan ancestor of Sigurd, the dragon-slayer of Norse mythology. Here was a he-man from Lugu Lake who could trace his ancestry to the Vikings of Norway, to a time when his forefather tribesmen hunted down and colonized Iceland, the Orkney Islands and Normandy. How these hulking Viking strongmen made their long way to the far mountains of Lugu Lake in China remains a mystery to me, but it might suggest why Zhaxi and his Mosuo brothers look so different from the Chinese and other ethnic minority groups in this part of the world. Inadvertently I may have stumbled across the Vikings of Asia.

More than Viking physicality, what is truly impressive about Mosuo men is how content and comfortable they are in their role as the peacock. I was intrigued by the phenomenon of the Mosuo peacock on my initial trip to Lugu Lake. There I was, paying two young brothers to row me across the lake to see a Buddhist temple on one of the nine little islands studded across the lake. While the younger 16-year-old paddled away, his older brother took the easier job of handling the rudder, all the while singing away. He tried very hard to look cool and sexy.

'So, you are practising your singing?' I asked casually.

'Yes,' he said, 'I have to be good at it. Don't you know, a Mosuo man has to look stylish and be good at singing and dancing if he is to get the girls? Tonight I will dress up and sing this song at the village fête. I hope my singing will catch the attention of this pretty girl I know.'

'Good luck!' I said, as I looked back at his brother still bearing the brunt of the rowing. When they deposited me back on shore, I decided to reward the harder-working lad with a fat 100-yuan tip.

Curiously enough, I bumped into the younger teenager at a local dress shop the following morning. He was there with his friends, shopping for a trinket for a girl.

'He is buying a token of love because he is going to find his first girl!' one of his friends said teasingly.

I smiled, silently congratulating myself for having facilitated this fledgling peacock's first foray into the world of the birds and the bees.

I suppose this anecdote tells me that Mosuo boys start young in their life-long flirting career. With practice they mature into experienced lady-killers by the time they reach their 30s, going by the chat I had with two young male friends on one of those interminably long road trips from Lijiang to Lugu Lake. We had time to kill, chatting about the weather, the forthcoming harvests and their varying careers as wait-ers, singers and tour-bus drivers. The conversation somehow veered to stories about their amorous love lives. I jumped at the chance to tease more details out of them.

'When did you start your love life?' was my first question.

'Eighteen,' said one.

'Seventeen,' the other quipped.

'Just how many episodes have you chalked up?' I asked the younger of the two, a 28-year-old who worked as a tour-bus driver and there-fore had lots of opportunity to meet all sorts of people. His reply was delivered in an unassuming tone.

'Not too many, probably only 70 to 80.'

A small count, perhaps? Pointing to his companion, who at 31 appeared more savvy and confident, he suggested that his older friend probably had a higher score.

'So, how many?' I asked the friend.

'Oh, let me think,' he said, staying silent for a few moments as he counted it all up in his head. Finally, the rejoinder came.

'More than 200, nearer to 300.'

'Wow! Impressive! Both of you!' I felt obliged to exclaim.

'So what do you look for in a woman?' was my next question.

'She has to be pretty,' came a quick reply, 'and be receptive.'

As the two young men rambled on, they gave me a glimpse of how a Mosuo peacock goes about his business. It emerged that the target of any flirting need not be a beauty. All that was needed was an interesting-looking woman, enough to arouse his interest. She might be younger, or older, it did not seem to matter. It was not necessary that she be all dressed up. Once spotted, the mark would have little escape. Without missing a step, he would begin the dance of the peacock, cajoling, preening, flirting. Oh, how he would flirt! The moment the peacock caught a woman's eyes, he would home in, locking his gaze on her.

The flirting styles might differ, but his forward manner would leave no doubt that he meant to flirt with her. A Mosuo man's favourite ruse is the gaze-deeply-into-the-eyes trick with an unmistakable twinkle in his eyes. Add to that a few touchy-feely moves and he would have completed his brazen-faced approach. If the target showed an interest, he would immediately jump at the opportunity. His next words would probably follow a simple script:

'What time tonight?'

'Where shall we meet?'

If the target showed no interest, it would be no big deal to the flirt. He would simply move on to the next target. I would not be wrong in saying that a Mosuo man never misses a beat when an opportunity arises to flirt with a woman. He almost always goes on automatic pilot to give it a try.

I am reminded of the story of how Gemu the Goddess is an inspiration to the Mosuo women on how to conduct their love lives. Interestingly the same is true for the Mosuo men, who also look to the flirtatious side of their female mountain deity as encouragement for their own amorous adventures.

For one who has done my fair share of flirting, and being flirted with, I have never received as many advances and open propositions as I have in the land of the Mosuo peacocks. Once, during a communal meal with a group of Mosuo friends, I sensed the young man across the table shooting the trademark deep gazing at me. It scared the daylights out of me. Another time, I had someone knocking softly but incessantly on my hotel room door for 20 minutes without stopping, hoping that I would let him in.

Gumi was with me at the market one day when she introduced me to a rather dull middle-aged farmer from her village. He came up to me, smiled and extended his hand to shake. I took his hand and to my surprise he did the three-stroke trick in the centre of my palm. I had heard about this trick, which is the Mosuo signal for 'How about it?' Three strokes back on the other palm would mean 'Yes'. I did not stroke back. A few months later the same man asked Gumi to deliver a message to me.

'He wanted me to tell you that he would like you to marry him,' Gumi said with a laugh.

'What did you tell him?' I said.

'I told him he will have to ask you himself,' she said with a laugh.

I received a more innovative twist on the Masonic handshake one night by the jetty when a handsome Mosuo man asked this of me:

'Give me your answer after I have finished skimming three pebbles across the lake.'

From my perspective as a woman much older than the 30-something Mosuo maidens, the experience of being flirted with so often is a refreshing change from the relatively 'flirt-less' existence in my other life in the city. I wish the men outside Lugu Lake, who for one reason or another are hesitant to be as barefaced as the Mosuo flirts, would learn from these village folk.

For all his macho mien, a Mosuo male is not one to shy away from a softer, 'feminine' side that a Chinese man would never go near in a million years.

One of the more endearing pageants I have seen in Mosuo family life is Xiao Liujing taking the greatest care to cradle and take care of his baby sister. I have witnessed similar scenes repeated many times over, telling me how natural it is for a Mosuo male to take on a nurturing role in looking after his younger siblings and relatives. It could well be that he is taught from early on to share in the 'womanly' role of caring for the babies and toddlers around the house.

Unlike boys I see in a village or city in China, the Mosuo boy does not grow up shunning the chore that is traditionally reserved for girls in a Chinese family. A Mosuo boy thinks nothing of carrying his baby sister or taking his toddler brother by the hand everywhere. The boy grows up imbued with this positive attitude to watching over the young. I was once made to wait before talking business with a Mosuo grandfather until he had bathed his twin granddaughters and changed their nappies.

What we view as the typically feminine trait of adorning ourselves is commonplace in the Mosuo man. He possesses a huge fondness for jewellery. Almost to a man, a Mosuo guy wears at least a couple of large rings on either or both hands, plus a (fake) ivory or bone bangle on his wrist. To complete the ensemble, he adds a small Buddhist amulet around his neck. On top of it all, he may have another larger neckpiece from which dangles a large animal tooth or a fancy tobacco pouch. The Mosuo man is more bedecked and bejewelled than the average Mosuo woman. On any other type of man, this gaudy get-up would look suspiciously unmasculine. Not on the Mosuo male, who carries it off with such aplomb that it does not seem to distract from his apparent manliness. He somehow manages to exude masculinity even in his peacock finery.

A macho Mosuo man will not think twice about getting down on the dance floor of a nightclub with another man. At first sight I found this phenomenon strangely interesting and certainly challenging for any man in the Chinese context. I put it down to yet another example of the never-say-die attitude of the Mosuos when it comes to having fun. Dancing with another man, or a bigger group of men, is perfectly acceptable in the social circle of these he-men.

One of the more interesting turn of events I have observed in this land of preening peacocks is the number of young men hoping to land a woman of some substance as a way out of what they perceive as less than comfortable circumstances in their home environment.

I know this young man who was reputed to be a truly well-practised seducer of women. He would sing and dance his way into many a woman's heart, especially if she was a city girl on a holiday to Lugu Lake. He finally landed a rich divorcee from Chengdu in the neighbouring province of Sichuan, whom he duly married. She proceeded to lavish love and money on her new man, helping him set up a restaurant, turning his mother's homestead into a hotel complex and buying him two cars. Another friend from Baju bought his first tourist bus with the help of a woman, also from Chengdu.

In a curious way, this is a reversal of the oft-heard story in Chinese cities where pretty young women employ their seductive skills in the hope of landing an older, rich man to take care of their needs. It is a familiar modern route travelled by women who depend on the wherewithal of men in male-dominated societies.

In the Kingdom of Women things are turned the other way round. In a society used to woman-headed households, with men having no direct and exclusive control over family resources, some of the men are tempted to look elsewhere if they want to strike out independently. Used to their role as the seed-waterer, they look around to find a receptive female audience from the outside world with whom they can plant a stake.

The modus operandi works for the Mosuo man. The same is not true for his Mosuo sisters. It does not seem necessary for the women. They have to continue being responsible for the maintenance of their female lineage and the sustenance of their family farms or businesses. They do not need the 'out' that some of their brothers seek. They see no need to become fortune seekers. They leave that to their brothers.

If the women are confident in their special place in matrilineal Mosuo society, the men too are confident in the role of playing the Romeo in this fun-seeking community. They are confident, knowing their place in society, embracing their masculinity like their unspoken mascot, the peacock.

9

A Marriage That Is
Not a Marriage

By far the most remarkable tale of the Mosuo tribe is their story of love. It is the way they conduct their love lives in an almost undreamt-of type of 'walking marriage'.

Walking marriage is the most talked of, most bandied about narrative to come out of the Mosuo way of life. Anthropologists and sociologists focus on the phenomenon, writers pen volumes on the subject and documentary filmmakers produce countless episodes on the theme. It is also the most misunderstood concept to come out of the Kingdom of Women.

Many writers call walking marriage free love, where each partner is not limited to just one sexual mate. On the other hand, some see it as open marriage. Others label it as polygamous, meaning more than one wife or husband at the same time, or polyandrous, implying a woman with more than one husband, or even polygynous, where a man has more than one wife.

In point of fact, none of these characterizations fits the concept of walking marriage. The 'marriage' part of the phrase is itself a misnomer. Mosuo walking marriage is no marriage at all, if we understand marriage to be a relationship between a husband and a wife, with the pair forming the core building block of a permanent nuclear family. Mosuo society has no notion of marriage and equally no conception of a 'husband' or a 'wife' within the family. The 'walking' or 'visiting' part of the phrase merely refers to the act of a man walking to or visiting a woman's place for a night of pleasure.

As a love story, walking marriage is unique and so different from marriage in patriarchal terms that it is impossible to make any direct comparison between the two. It has to be understood on its own terms, within its own parallel universe. It took me years before I got my head around its meaning and manifestations.

A good place to start is to use the correct nomenclature. Instead of using the well-worn 'walking marriage' or 'visiting marriage', I will at times use the original word from the Mosuo language, referring to the 'visit' as *sese* (pronounced as 'say-say'). Stripped of its romanticism, *sese* in its raw form is what a woman and a man do together in private. When one drills down to the basics, *sese* between the sexes is not much different from romancing elsewhere. It is the different ways of expressing sexual liaison by the Mosuo that is worth the telling.

During my first stay in a Mosuo bed-and-breakfast inn, I was pleased to be invited to an after-dinner chat with the family by the hearth. Holding court in the family room was the grandmother. With her were her two grown-up daughters, one in her 40s and the other in her 30s. The grandmother introduced me to her two teenage grandchildren, born of the elder daughter, and a year-old toddler, born to the younger daughter. As we sipped tea, a middle-aged man arrived on his motorbike and joined us for tea. He exchanged pleasantries with the grandmother but did not bother with the teenagers or the baby. Just then, the younger daughter stood up to leave the room with the man, directing an instruction to her teenage niece.

'Look after the little one, will you?'

The teenager nodded. Her aunt walked out of the room, followed by the man, and I could hear their footsteps traipsing up the wooden stairs outside, likely on their way to her room. It dawned on me that the man must have been her *axia*, and they were in a walking-marriage relationship.

Because the woman's *axia* did not have any interaction with her toddler the whole time he was sitting with us in the family room, I figured that he probably had nothing to do with her child. He could not have been the father from the way he acted. But I did not dare to venture a question. Any book on the Mosuos should carry a forewarning that it is thought highly impolite to delve into a Mosuo's love life.

I raised an eyebrow to myself, pleased that I had come so close to witnessing an episode of *sese* in real time. It was rare to catch something so private that even family members are usually kept from the secret, at least in the early stages of one's walking marriage.

When a woman decides to take a new lover, her casual one-night stand or fledgling liaison is always conducted in full secret. She and her *axia* try very hard to hide their *nana sese*, the furtive *sese*, when the man visits her home. The place of assignation is always the woman's home, never the man's. Obviously I could never bear witness to any of this, but I understand that an *axia* spends the night in the woman's own 'flower chamber' at home, a room given to her when she comes of age.

In a typical Mosuo home the flower chamber of each of the daughters is located on the second floor in a different wing by the courtyard, away from the grandmother's room. It is each woman's private space where she can do as she pleases, including conducting her assignations in secret.

Although each *axia* assignation is kept from the prying eyes of family members and any outsider, the Mosuo is quite unabashed when depicting the furtive *sese* scene in every song-and-dance skit performed for tourists.

The light dims on the stage set as the audience see a man in a hat creeping towards the outside of a Mosuo house. A woman's face appears at the window on the second floor. She listens out in the quiet night for the man to throw three pebbles against her windowpane, the signal they agreed on when they met earlier. We see her looking back to make sure no one else is around as she treads softly to open the window to let in her visitor. He quickly scales the wall to reach her window, and as she kisses him he climbs into the flower chamber and hangs his hat on the doorknob.

The light in the room dims again as the couple kiss, and we see another hatted man stealthily walking up to the door, his hand poised to knock. He steps back in shock, realizing there is another hat on the knob. Hanging his head in dejection, he walks away from the flower chamber, knowing that his rival has beaten him to it. Everyone claps at this point in the dramatized version of *nana sese* between the first pair of *axias*, with a sub-plot of another man waiting in the wings to suggest the possibility of a revolving door for another *axia*.

The second act starts with the same backdrop, but this time at the crack of dawn as the crowing of a cock is heard over the sound system. The window opens once more and we see the man kiss his *axia* goodbye, climb over the sill to slide down to the ground and steal away in the dim light of the dawning day. We all stand up to applaud and leave, recognizing that this is the end of the story of one night in the life of a pair of Mosuo *axias* doing their *nana sese* thing.

The play-acting is probably a close approximation of walking marriage in its unembellished, furtive form. It is the equivalent of a casual one-night stand. The two Mosuo lads I mentioned in the last chapter would count each of their exaggerated number of *axia* encounters as *nana sese* of the furtive kind. Indulging in *nana sese* is common-place among the Mosuos. Everyone, woman or man, does it, especially when they are young. Even Gemu the goddess is an adherent of the practice with the other minor mountain gods while being committed to her long-term mountain god *axia*.

'Walking marriage is not all one-night-stands, you know,' said a woman friend when we sat down to discuss the subject. 'Like me, many of us have the same *axia* over time. I have been with my *axia* all my adult life.'

An *axia* pair may decide to go on meeting on a regular basis that progresses over time into a stable relationship, and this is when their affair is more open, with the 'walking' man not hiding his presence in front of the woman's family, like the man who visited the innkeeper's daughter at the bed and breakfast I visited.

The male *axia* comes and goes openly, though still only at night, in an arrangement the Mosuos view as an 'open' or 'conspicuous' visit, *gepie sese* in their language. Once out in the open, there is no need to keep the relationship secret any more. Middle-aged people are usually content to settle down with just one long-term *axia* in the *gepie sese* type of bonding over the long term.

I know a kindly gentle gardener in his 60s whom we all call Apu, or grandfather, who has been in a *gepie sese* relationship with his life-long *axia*. The notable thing about his walking marriage is that he continues to live in his own matrilineal homestead with his sister and her children, but on most days he is to be found in his *axia*'s own matrilineal home just a stone's throw away. While Apu has had only one *axia* over the last four decades, he is happy to commute between his bi-locale residences.

As I thought more about this enigmatic form of conducting one's love life, it became clear to me that the arrangement between Gumi and Gizi was another kind of *sese* love. Here was a pair of *axias* who decided to set up home together when Gumi's mother bequeathed her a plot of land.

In the last 20 years, Gumi and her man have built a home for themselves and produced my two godchildren. Their union appears to be permanent. I plucked up enough courage one day to broach the subject with Gumi.

'Did you get married to Gizi?'

'No,' Gumi said, 'there is no need to. It's all right this way.'

I understood then that theirs is still a walking-marriage arrangement and not a legal one, and of a type known as *ti dzi ji mao the* to the Mosuo, meaning an *axia* pair cohabiting together, socially accepted by the community as a couple.

I looked around my friends and found more variations of walking marriage. My buddy Jizuo, brother number six in Gumi's family, had lived with his adoptive mother in her maternal home all his life. With only the two of them and no younger woman at home, they decided the best solution was to have his *axia* move in and be 'adopted' by the family. With a young woman in the house, the family had a chance to continue the bloodline of his adoptive mother. When the couple produced two lovely daughters, they made sure to name them after Jizuo's adoptive mother's home name, Hansa, thus 'forcing' a continuance of her matrilineage. The Mosuo would call this type of arrangement *ji the ti dzi*.

Sometimes it works the other way round. When Erchima inherited her choice piece of land in Lige, she needed a man around the house to provide the much needed muscle for the heavy work to come. This was when Zhaxi, her *axia*, moved into her home, although in this case he was not formally 'adopted' by Erchima's maternal family. He retains his own family name and is not considered as belonging to Erchima's maternal lineage when it comes to family business. Only maternal family members and 'adopted' *axias* have speaking rights in these matters.

The unique thing about the love life of the Mosuo is the total absence of marriage. Mosuos simply do not get married. Women and men do not pair up as husband and wife, whether socially or legally. Even when they stay together for a lifetime, they are not 'married' as the rest of the world understands the term. Theirs is a society with neither husbands nor wives.

As far as I am aware, nowhere else in the world is there a society that exists without marriage. In the traditional marriage-less world of the Mosuo, a woman and a man never form a nuclear family with the aim of creating a separate unit consisting of themselves and their children. In their parallel universe, the 'nuclear' family is a separate unit consisting of the grandmother and her children and all her matrilineal descendants. *Axias*, who may be husbands or wives in our universe, need not apply for membership in this family.

In the context of love without the restraint of marriage, it is understandably easy for each Mosuo person to feel free to seek out as many or as few lovers as she or he wishes.

A Mosuo has a menu of choices on how to lead her or his love life. A person is free to choose to have an *axia* furtively, openly, adopted into the family, or as a couple, with or without a marriage certificate. Additionally, such choice is not necessarily a once-in-a-lifetime option. The choice is open, any time, many times, serially, contemporaneously, at any stage of one's life, to be exercised at will, and the permutations of the choices can be limitless. No one is criticized for whichever variation of *sese* she or he chooses.

'I practise walking marriage,' the grandmother of a friend whom I met for the first time said simply and openly when I asked her about her family.

Another woman friend of mine comes from a large family of seven siblings, all sired by the long-term *axia* of their mother. I know each and every one of her sisters and brothers, and so was at a loss when my friend introduced someone else as her sister.

'I don't remember ever meeting her at your house,' I said innocently.

'Oh, we call her sister because my father was an *axia* of her mother a long time ago.'

So even a man in a long-term *sese* relationship can have *nana sese* on the side. I began to understand the idea that to a Mosuo another short-term lover now and then would not invalidate the relationship between a person and her or his long-term *axia*.

In this milieu where everyone has freedom of choice, a Mosuo is sure to have a healthy attitude towards love and sex. Love is free and often frequent. Love is also freed from the many social and religious restrictions that exist in the rest of the world that holds marriage as the cornerstone of the family. As to be expected, the Mosuos have none of the inhibitions familiar to the rest of us.

There was just one more variation on the theme that I wanted to explore, and I raised the subject at a male drinking session that I gate-crashed.

'Do Mosuos practise gay love?' I asked in a nonchalant manner.

'You are kidding!' exclaimed the loudest voice among the men, followed by the biggest guffaws I had ever heard.

Back to the heterosexual world of the Mosuos, they do not entangle themselves in the numerous courting rituals found in other cultures. At the heart of it, and I have seen plenty of evidence to prove this, the Mosuo mode of seduction is stripped of all the preliminaries of 'dating' as we know it. No one is expected to spend time and effort to seduce. There are no obligatory three dinner dates or the more formal marriage proposal before making someone an *axia*. The Mosuo man is unlike his Chinese counterpart who demands good housekeeping skills in a woman or insists on a virgin to share his wedding bed in case his baby turns out to be another man's progeny.

What comes across as a total surprise is that the freedom to choose is available to both women and men. Equally. This is surprising when we are looking in from the outside patriarchal world but the Mosuo would have it no other way. After all, this is the Kingdom of Women.

'Just how many sexual partners does a Mosuo typically have?' a young male friend visiting Lugu Lake asked me. This question invariably comes up whenever I talk about Mosuo love with a visitor.

'The statistics vary depending on which sociology book you read,' is my usual evasive answer.

Some scholars say that a Mosuo woman's batting average is about four to five *axias* in her lifetime. Others put the figure higher. Most credit the Mosuo man with a much higher count, at least from ten upwards. I am told that mathematically speaking it is an impossibility for the female and the male averages to be different from each other if the population base remains the same. If so, the respective figures for both women and men must be somewhere in between, about eight to nine. This is a respectable count by any measure. Whatever the number, the headcount may not be as important as the fact that having several sexual partners over a lifetime is a normal, acceptable part of Mosuo life.

I know a grandmother with five grown-up children whose *sese* history is fairly typical of the stories I have collected on Mosuo women. Each of her children bore only a slight resemblance to each other, if at all, suggesting to me that she might have had different *axias* during her various pregnancies. I did not probe the question openly with her but she gave me a clue when I told her that I was the godmother to Gumi's daughter in Baju village.

'Then we are related to each other,' she said, without offering any more information.

Piqued, I asked Gumi about the possible family connection.

'Her *axia* at the time her youngest son was born was an uncle in my mother's family.'

Later I pieced together the story of this Mosuo grandmother. She had a total of four *axias* in her life, with the first of whom she bore two girls, the second a son, the third another girl, and finally the fourth my putative godbrother.

Her story of multiple *axias* would certainly raise the hackles of a red-blooded Chinese man who would have grown up with the standard patriarchal narrative that only men are polygamous, the women being natural monogamists. As such, a man is entitled to have as many wives and concubines as he likes. The issue of a woman's entitlement to do the same with someone other than her husband does not even merit a mention.

Anyone who has visited the Forbidden City, home to generations of Chinese emperors in Beijing, will have walked through the women's wing of the ancient palace that in its heyday housed hundreds of imperial concubines waiting to be picked at a day's notice to share the emperor's bed.

My own father shared the same sentiment as the emperors of old China. A successful entrepreneur, he had the means and opportunity to set up multiple homes with different mistresses in every port where he did business, while we lived at home with my mother, his first wife. And his is not the only example I can think of in recalling the many real-life stories of how Chinese men act on what they see as male prerogative.

It was entirely different for Chinese women. I remember my own grandmother telling me how a married woman in feudal times would face a terrible fate if she were ever found in bed with another man. Her crime would have been thought so vile and offensive to her husband's authority over her that she would bring the wrath of the neighbourhood upon her. The villagers would force her and her adulterous lover into a bamboo pig cage each and throw them into the river to test their innocence. If they struggled free of the cage and swam to the surface of the water, they would be declared innocent. If not, they were guilty and deserved to die for their transgression.

Returning to the concept of *sese* relationships, I find it refreshing to see little evidence of a Mosuo person treating an *axia* as 'hers' or 'his'. No *axia* belongs exclusively to her or him sexually. No one thinks of an *axia* as a possession. All this makes sense in the framework of a society without marriage and without the bonds binding a man and a woman exclusively in fidelity as husband and wife. The Mosuo model makes sense in the context of a matrilineal family structure that freezes out the outsider *axia* as a member.

At the heart of the love life of the Mosuo, every person, woman or man, is free to choose a sexual partner any time. No one 'belongs' to another; therefore one is free to have one or more partners, whether at the same time or serially over time. An *axia* is only an *axia* when the pair 'visit' together. In fact, the classical meaning of an *axia* is a lover at the time she or he is sleeping with that lover. The moment the man walks away from the flower chamber, the *axia* relationship is ended. If that same person comes back as a lover, he becomes an *axia* once again.

Although many outsiders may view Mosuo love life as free and open, it is really not 'open' for all to see. To the Mosuos, love, although given and received freely, needs to be shrouded behind a veil of secrecy. The coupling is conducted in secret and remains undeclared to others in most cases. Even with *axias* who are acknowledged long-term partners, the couple would never overtly display the fact in public. A Mosuo woman is too shy to admit that she is involved with someone. She does not talk about it and does not go about town parading her *axia*.

Being shy about one's love life is not merely a function of modesty. Every Mosuo is taught from a young age never to evoke the subject of sex in front of elders or relatives of the opposing gender. It is all right when girls get together to banter about their *axias*, but I have been told many a time to hush up when I forget the rule and tell a blue joke in front of a group of friends who happen to be sisters and brothers or female and male cousins.

Because the Mosuos shield their *axia* relationships from the public eye, it is often difficult to spot a Mosuo couple by outward appearances. When I wander into town, I seldom see a Mosuo couple whom I know to be *axias* walking together side by side. Instead I see women hanging out with other women, and men hanging about with other men. A woman goes to market with her female relatives and friends but will rarely be seen walking about with her *axia* in tow. In the good old days an *axia* couple might continue their relationship without any public display of affection or public knowledge of their pairing. I have befriended many a Mosuo woman and man at different times and it would take me months or even years before I learnt just who has been a particular person's *axia* all along.

Going about as a couple is not the thing to do socially. The Mosuo view of limited coupledom is at the opposite end of the spectrum that focuses on the two-halves-of-a-whole ideal that we find in contemporary society. More than forbearing to put a ring on the fourth finger, a Mosuo seldom refers to 'we' when talking about her or his *axia*. Rather than being confronted in a one-on-one conversation with endless references to 'we' in a world filled with in-your-face coupledom, I feel much less intimidated by the milder Mosuo approach.

For much of the time a Mosuo person goes about everyday living independently of the *axia*. The two lives of a pair of *axias* are far from being lived in tandem, certainly never on a 24/7 basis. I have never encountered an *axia* checking on the whereabouts of a partner or telephoning the partner to see what she or he is doing. Just as an *axia* has no exclusive claim on the affection of a partner, the *axia* does not claim any entitlement to the time and physical presence of that partner.

It is almost as if each of them goes her or his own way until it is time to see each other at night or help each other in some common household or farm chore. On more than one occasion, I would ask a friend where her *axia* was when I noticed that he was not around.

'I don't know. Out somewhere on a family matter,' would come the reply. Of course, in referring to family she would have meant the maternal family of her *axia*, not hers, implying that it was not something that concerned her.

All roads lead back to the matrilineal family in the Mosuo way of life. A person's matrilineal family takes precedence over anything to do with the *axia*. I have come across so many instances when a Mosuo friend would never question or object to her *axia* taking time to attend to his own family business. To the last, family has the first claim over a Mosuo's life. One's own maternal family comes above all others and no *axia* has any prior claim to that. Whenever something crops up in the family, be it a celebration, an illness of a relative or a death in the family, I have again and again witnessed a Mosuo person immediately dropping everything and rising to the call, with no question ever being asked by the *axia*. No *axia* would dream of asking about the whys and the wherefores of the event, because the *axia* knows that she or he has no right to do so. Being part of a couple does not give the *axia* any prior rights ahead of the other's maternal family precisely because the *axia* is not counted as family.

It follows that it is no simple matter to figure out which of a woman's children her current *axia* is the father of or, indeed, whether he is the father of any of them. The odds are that a woman's children may have been fathered by different *axias* over time. Nevertheless, in her eyes and those of her family and community, all her offspring belong to her matrilineal family, and that is enough for them. The issue of who is the father of a child simply does not come up. It does not need to come up because the male progenitor of a child is irrelevant in a society that measures lineage strictly according to the matrilineal bloodline.

I learnt just how irrelevant a 'father' is from observing the close relationship between a friend of mine and her next-door neighbour in Baju. The two women friends do a lot of things together, planting and harvesting rice for each other, celebrating their children's coming of age, even going on weekly shopping trips to town. To each other, they see themselves as close friends. Never do they or their relatives acknowledge that they are 'related' to each other.

'Do you know that my neighbour is sort of related to me?' my friend confided in me one day. 'When her mother gave birth to her, her *axia* was my brother.'

In our patriarchal world of fathers and husbands, my friend would be an aunt to her neighbour, who in turn would be her niece. In their matriarchal world without fathers and husbands, my friend's brother as an *axia* was not relevant to either the neighbour's family or my friend's family, and so the two women carry on as friends, not relatives.

While fatherhood does not figure in a Mosuo family, this does not mean that a male *axia* who has helped propagate a child is disregarded entirely. The mother and grandmother of the child and probably her *axia* of the moment know of his connection with the child. Even the community may have an inkling of the identity of the putative water bearer.

'I think that young man sitting there may be the son of so-and-so in the village,' an older woman said to me, 'Don't you think he looks exactly like so-and-so?'

The Mosuos have a word for father, 'Abu'. However, Abu has none of the obligations and responsibilities incumbent on fatherhood in a patriarchal setting. A child of Abu belongs to the mother's family, and Abu has no claim over the child. He does not have to provide for or look after the child. The mother and her matrilineal family do that. Abu's identity is not needed to validate the societal status of the mother or the child. The mother and her family do that too.

Given the insignificant place given to Abu in Mosuo family life, I seldom hear a Mosuo talking about her or his father, at least among the older generations. I have been advised not to ask openly about the identity of a father unless the information has been volunteered. It is not unusual for a Mosuo not to know the identity of her or his father and it is considered impolite to pry into their mother's privacy and the history of her personal life. This privacy regarding one's *axia*, or *axias*, as the case may be, is so deeply ingrained among the Mosuos that it is never referred to in polite company.

A Mosuo man has three options open to him when he becomes Abu to a child. Like my friend's brother in relation to the neighbour, he can ignore his progeny altogether. Both Abu and daughter ignore each other on the street.

Alternatively, an Abu can choose to acknowledge his child, bringing presents on special occasions such as the New Year and the child's coming-of-age celebration. A nephew of Gumi does just that when he makes an appearance in Baju to see his son born to an earlier *axia* of his.

Or the Abu can take on the full mantle of fatherhood, especially when he is still romantically involved with the mother, as in the case of Zhaxi who cohabits with Erchima and their two children. He is as good as a father in a patriarchal home, providing for his children and looking after them in every aspect of their lives.

None of these three courses of action is imposed by Mosuo mores. The male Mosuo is at liberty to choose the path with which he is most comfortable, with no stigma attached to his choice.

When I look at the overall scheme of things, I do not see the Mosuos ranking their love lives very high up in the scale of family life. While they recognize human sexuality for what it is, that it is natural for a woman and a man to have sex together, and celebrate it by giving complete freedom to people to indulge in it, they never elevate it into the be-all and end-all of human existence. Sexual love may be crucial for the survival of their tribe but it is not the glue that links a family together. Love, for the Mosuo, may be more than one, but it is private and most certainly comes way below family.

The centre of their lives is the matrilineal family and everything else, including *sese*, is subsumed under its core. At best, *sese* is an appendage to the matrilineal family, and that is the place it holds in Mosuo society. I am aware that this may seem untenably strange for a society that preaches free love, but that is the only way I can reconcile all the ramifications thrown up by the complications involved in *sese* life.

Personally I have come round to accepting that walking marriage makes logical sense in putting human sexuality in its correct place in our lives. I think sex is a human condition with a thousand variations in its expression that cannot, and should not, be confined within the narrow space allotted to it in most societies. I cannot buy into the fallacy that sex has to be limited to one partner over a lifetime. I certainly reject the straightjacket imposed by the prescription that a wife and husband must obey a lifelong pledge to each other of sexual fidelity and exclusivity. And I most certainly repudiate the false paternalistic notion that women are monogamous while men are polygamous. If we are honest with ourselves as human beings, we know deep down that there is really no one person in the world who could satisfy our every need. To me, the Mosuos have got it right in extolling sex as a happy, natural requisite and placing it in the right place as an addendum to family life.

Still, most people in China and perhaps the rest of mankind, I fear, may disagree with me, and probably think that the Mosuos live very much on the wild and unacceptably sinful side of life. It may be asking too much of them to take the blinkers off and see their uni-world view as but one variation of human society and appreciate the possibility of diversity offered by the Mosuo way of *sese* life.

10

The Matrilineal Ties
That Bind

Knowing how to navigate around a three-generation Mosuo family is one thing, but getting to the heart of understanding all the intricate matrilineal ties that bind their family is quite another. There is much more that meets the eye, and the challenge it poses has tested my cultural sensitivity and intellectual curiosity to a degree I had not known before.

Even the immediate family setup was baffling. At one level I understood that a large matrilineal family of three generations lived together as a unit, with all its members sharing the same female bloodline. To recap, the family of the first generation has the grandmother as head, with one or two of her brothers sitting alongside as co-heads; the second generation consists of all her daughters and sons; and the third generation includes all the children of her daughters only. I wondered how such a family in identifying itself to the community would differ from the way my patrilineal Chinese family identified itself.

Like all Chinese families, we adopt our father's paternal surname as our surname. But unlike many other societies which put surnames at the end of their given names, a Chinese person wears the male family surname proudly at the very front of her name: thus Choo WaiHong, with Choo, my father's surname, coming first. Putting the definitive paternal surname in front of my given name, WaiHong, speaks volumes about the importance of the male bloodline in my Chinese heritage.

'Can I see your identity card, please?' I asked a Mosuo friend, Cher-er, trying to find out her surname.

'Here,' she said, as she handed it to me, in the casual way a person in China would treat her national identity paper used for everything, everywhere.

I found to my surprise that Cher-er's name had six Chinese characters to it, compared to my much shorter, typical Chinese three-character name. I knew her full Mosuo given name was Cher-er Lazuo, and found the four characters at the end of her six-part name. Mosuo given names are like that, long and commonly made up of two compound names strung together, making it a four-syllable given name. My friend's full name on the identity card read 'Laker Cher-er Lazuo'.

'Are the first two characters your surname?' I asked.

'No,' she said, 'we Mosuos don't have a surname like you have. The first two characters, Laker, are my home name.'

'What do you mean by "home name"?'

'My home name is the name of the place where my mother's family lives,' she explained.

I found out that the home name is usually the name of the place chosen by an earlier generation of the particular Mosuo maternal family, or is sometimes the name of its earliest female ancestor, the name being carried on down the generations belonging to the female bloodline. Every daughter and son of the same mother and of the mother's sisters, and so on, bear the same home name over the generations.

In a way, it is similar to the concept of a patrilineal surname, except that in the case of the Mosuo it is the matrilineal 'home name' belonging to the mother that is used. And the home name is also placed in front of the given name like the Chinese, except that, for the Mosuo, this highlights the importance of the female bloodline in Mosuo society.

Everyone keeps the home name of her or his maternal bloodline because of the matrilineal ties that bind. No one changes her or his home name to brand herself or himself as belonging to another family unrelated to the original maternal bloodline, least of all the home name of an *axia*.

Although Cher-er Lazuo is cohabiting with her *axia* as a couple in their own farmstead, she has not changed her home name 'Laker' to her *axia*'s home name after pairing up with him. Her *axia* equally keeps his own maternal home name even after moving in with Cher-er. So it is difficult to tell if a person is an *axia* of another just by knowing their full names, since neither will rename themselves with her or his *axia*'s home name. They keep their own home name for life, with one exception.

The exception is when a person is 'adopted' formally into a matrilineal family, like my friend Jizuo, the older brother of Gumi. Jizuo, having been given away to his maternal aunt at birth, had changed his home name from that used by Gumi and the rest of his original matrilineal family to the home name of his aunt, Hansa. Ever since his official adoption into this other matrilineal family, he has dropped the home name of Gumi's direct matrilineal bloodline and identified himself as a Hansa, of his maternal aunt's line.

Whenever I walk into a Mosuo home, I can immediately sense the feminist vibes, to use a modern-day term. Matrilineage matters in the home. I have already talked about Gumi's strong presence as the owner-cum-manager-cum-chief financial officer of her farm, and Erchima's key role in the running of the Zhaxi Guesthouse.

Both Gumi's and Erchima's mother before them also took charge of everything to do with their homes, from farming to managing the domesticated animals, housekeeping, cooking, cleaning, sewing and tending to the young and the sick. These may be considered lowly 'housewife' duties in a Chinese patriarchal home, but Mosuo society does not disparage nor undervalue these functions. The role of the women is instead played up and remains undiminished. In their world, these functions are crucial and pivotal to their lives, leaving intact the prime position of women.

The woman's role is primary; the role of the men in carrying out the heavy manual work needed around the household, as well as in liaising with the community outside the home, is secondary. To me, this is a most interesting *volte-face* of roles. The men being in charge of the seemingly important task of external relations does not elevate them to a higher position in the female pyramidal social structure. The men accept their secondary role and will never question the authority of the matriarch.

The matriarch enjoys her pivotal role when she is young and strong, but in her declining years she will need to pass the reins over to one of her daughters. The Aha grandmother I knew had given up the headship position to her third daughter and not her firstborn daughter, as I would have expected. I had assumed that seniority of birth mattered, in the same way that my Chinese patriarchal family thought the world of my brother, the eldest child and the first male to be born in my generation.

'Why is your youngest daughter running the farm and not your eldest daughter?' I asked the Aha matriarch.

'Simple,' she said. 'My youngest daughter is the most able and intelligent of my three daughters.'

In a snub to the concept of female primogeniture, if there is one, the more egalitarian Mosuo grandmother, in choosing the successor to her matriarchy, places faith in merit. More significantly, the successor is always a daughter, never a son, confirming once again that inside every Mosuo home beats a woman's heart.

Taking an inside look at a three-generation matrilineal family, I am cognizant of the fact that only the children, counting both girls and boys, born to the grandmother's daughters make up the third generation because the grandmother's bloodline can only run through the veins of her daughters. The children of grandmother's sons are never counted as part of her family because they are born of other women not sharing the grandmother's bloodline.

In practice it is bewildering to see just how deep the bloodline theory expresses itself in the dynamics between the maternally related family members of the second generation of daughters and the children of the daughters in the third generation.

Starting with the core matrilineal principle that each and every family member is related by a common female bloodline, a family treats all the children of all the daughters as full-blooded sisters and brothers of each other. The entire third generation of children are primarily related as full siblings sharing the same consanguineous lineage.

'My sister wants to talk to you,' Xiao Zhaxi, the son of Erchima said to me one day. I thought he was referring to his younger sister, the swimmer athlete studying in Kunming.

'Shall I call your sister long distance?' I said.

'No, not that sister. It's Ladhu, my older sister, the one in Lige,' he said.

'You have an older sister in Lige?' I asked, knowing he only had one sister younger than him.

'Yes, Ladhu. She is the daughter of my mother's older sister,' he said.

This came as a revelation. To my way of thinking, Ladhu is Xiao Zhaxi's maternal cousin, not his sister. But in the Mosuo scheme of things, Ladhu is his sister precisely because she and he are full-blooded siblings born to the same generation of two of the daughters of his grandmother's family. Ladhu, the daughter of Xiao Zhaxi's maternal aunt, and he, the son of Erchima, the sister of that maternal aunt, view each other as true-blood sister and brother, not as cousins. Both of them trace their common bloodline directly to their mothers' mother, the grandmother of them all.

If all the offspring of all the daughters of the grandmother are full-blood siblings, it is understandable that the children refer to their respective mother and all their maternal aunts as 'mother'. All the daughters of the grandmother are mothers to all the children in the big matrilineal household.

I continued my conversation with Xiao Zhaxi to probe this reference to multiple mothers.

'Which of your mother's sisters is the mother of your sister (cousin) Ladhu?' I asked.

'My Second Mother,' he replied.

'Your "second mother"?' I asked incredulously.

'Yes, she is my Second Mother because she is the second daughter of my grandmother. You know my mother, Erchima, is the fifth daughter of a family of seven daughters. The first daughter, being the eldest, is my Big Mother,' he said.

'So you call all the others mother? Like Third Mother, Fourth Mother, and so on?'

'Yes.'

'What do you call your own mother?'

'Mother.'

'And what do you call the youngest sister of Erchima?'

'Small Mother.'

Strange to us but it is common to hear a Mosuo making reference to a particular numbered mother among the other mothers. I can also

166

catch the nuances when a Mosuo pays respect to any of her or his mothers, similar to the way respect is due to her or his own mother.

From the perspective of the second generation of the grandmother's daughters, they each consider herself as a 'mother' to all the children born of herself and her sisters.

'My daughter Ladhu just had her second baby,' Erchima said of the same Ladhu, the daughter of her second sister.

In daily life, when someone tells me that her mother is across the street, I cannot help but wonder if she means her birth mother or one of her mother's sisters. In the same vein, if a friend points to someone as her brother, that person may be her brother born of the same mother or a brother born of her mother's sister. Based on their mode of reference, I cannot immediately tell just who is whose offspring without learning the full family background. Nor need I try to make the distinction. It is enough to know that they are simply full-blood relatives of the same generation sharing the same maternal lineage.

There is one more matrilineal tie to unravel. Often a Mosuo friend would tell me someone here or over there was a sister or a brother. Baffled, I would blink in disbelief as I would not recognize that person as one of her siblings, all of whom I have met.

'How is it that I have not met that sister of yours?' I would ask.

'Oh, my sister over there is the granddaughter of my grandmother's sister,' my friend would simply say, leaving me to figure it out.

That 'sister' of my friend is a sort of third or fourth cousin by my reckoning if hers was a patrilineal family. It is not. So although that 'sister' is further removed from my friend's immediate three-generational maternal family, to my friend, she is still a much closer relative than my far-removed cousin would have been. By my friend's reckoning, her 'sister' belongs to the same generation of those carrying her grandmother's bloodline, which means that both of them are the granddaughters of grandmothers sharing yet the same bloodline, and therefore sisters. The two women are in effect sisters to one another for the very reason that they share the same direct matrilineal lineage.

More recent times have seen a change to this stucture of real mothers and true siblings that appears to conflict with the matrilineal principle. I think it is due to the younger Mosuos having to deal with the different, patrilineal, concepts inherent in Chinese terminology used to describe family ties when they learn to speak Mandarin at school.

All language is loaded with the underlying philosophical foundations distinctive of its culture, and the Chinese language is no different. Mandarin and the other Chinese dialects display a heavy bias towards the prevailing patriarchal culture, using different terms to describe family relations belonging to the male-dominant bloodline and to distinguish them from the less important maternal connections.

For instance, in my family with two paternal uncles on my father's side, I use a special terminology to address my paternal cousins. I call my paternal cousin who is the eldest son of my father's eldest brother 'Tang Ker', the 'Tang' meaning the closest degree of family relationship based on the male bloodline of my family. 'Ker' simply means elder brother. It is similar to the Mosuo custom of calling a cousin a brother, except that the prefix 'Tang' makes it very clear that this cousin is a cousin on the male side of the family.

On the other hand, I refer to my maternal cousins with the prefix 'Biao', so my elder maternal boy cousin is 'Biao Ker' to me, the 'Biao' being the specific reference to the lesser, maternal side of things. Likewise there is one Chinese term for a paternal uncle or aunt and a different term for a maternal uncle or aunt.

The paternalistic terminology of the Chinese language is used everywhere in Chinese communities and will form part of any novel or textbook read by a student in a school teaching in the Chinese language.

Today's Mosuo youth will similarly be exposed to Chinese terminology differentiating between paternal and maternal relations.

When a Mosuo is speaking in Mandarin to outsiders such as me, she sometimes falls into the habit of borrowing the Chinese terms to describe her complicated family connections. In doing so, she will not be aware that the paternalistic terms cannot be translated directly into Mosuo. In trying to connect the dots between the Chinese world of paternal/maternal differentiations and the Mosuo world of only matrilineal relations, a Mosuo may inadvertently and unthinkingly add to her immediate matrilineal family a whole new set of paternal relatives which hitherto have never existed.

I have seen this happen on occasion in conversations with my Mosuo friends.

'Meet my sister,' a friend who comes from a matrilineal family of nine siblings said when introducing a total stranger to me.

'A tenth sibling in your family?' I asked in confusion after the stranger left us.

'Well, my father went with her mother who then gave birth to this woman. I call her my sister,' she said. 'In fact, I have another "sister" born of another woman with whom my father also had a walking-marriage relationship. So I have two additional sisters, sort of, in addition to my own family of nine sisters and brothers.'

These two 'sisters' of my friend are her half-sisters, if we adopt the paternalistic term to denote children sired by the same father with different women. It is strange to me that my friend broke two fundamental Mosuo principles in referring to them as her 'sisters'.

The first principle broken is that a relative is only a relation if she carries the same maternal bloodline. Neither 'sister' in this scenario had that qualification under the Mosuo system because each of them, as well as my friend, was born of a different woman and therefore did not share the same female bloodline.

The second principle broken is that the bloodline of the 'father' of any child is never taken into account when deciding on the matrilineal ties of a Mosuo person. The 'father' could not possibly pass on any meaningful blood ties of the matrilineal kind.

My Mosuo friend was wrong on both counts when she referred to the two would-be half-sisters as her 'sisters'. I think she was wrong because she unwittingly borrowed from the concepts inbuilt into Chinese terminology extolling the patrilineal bloodline as the mainspring of family life. She was thinking in the Chinese language, adding fatherhood and male blood relatives to her understanding of family life.

If she had resorted to the Mosuo language, she would have been unable to find any Mosuo term to describe the other offspring of the man who had been the *axia* of her mother, as being her 'sister' or even her 'half-sister'. The entire lexicon of Mosuo words for denoting relatives connected by the maternal bloodline outnumber those related to the male side of things by at least 13 to one. One list appearing in a recently published Chinese book on the Mosuo matrilineal system has 68 terms for relatives on the maternal side and only five for relatives of the *axia* who has contributed his genes to the offspring of a woman.

Inconsequential though the outsider male *axia* may be in a matrilineal household, there is still the danger of incest occurring between an unsuspecting pair of lovers. The Mosuo, like most other societies, have a clear taboo against incest, prohibiting sexual relations between sisters and brothers sharing the same maternal bloodline. The taboo extends further to cover a woman or man having sex with an *axia* who happens to share the same father, notwithstanding the Mosuo edict that the paternal bloodline counts for nothing in a matrilineal home. This could be attributed to a native, unschooled notion that something is not quite right about this kind of sexual liaison.

This two-pronged taboo has been worked out within the logic of Mosuo matrilineage. The first prong, between sisters and brothers related by the same matrilineal bloodline, is easy enough to enforce. As for the second prong, between a woman and a potential male *axia* whose mother is known to have shared the same man as the woman's mother, it is left to the woman's family to police.

If it so happens that a daughter shows an interest in a potential partner, the daughter's mother or grandmother will sound a word of caution, politely suggesting to the daughter that it is not a good idea to go with that man. In the reverse situation, where the young person about to start a walking marriage is a son, the male elder in the family, either the uncle or great uncle of the house, will sound the warning bell. In each case, no one crosses the Mosuo red line and raises the subject of sex with a relative of the opposite gender.

The young person is expected to heed the warning. As the potential *axia*'s mother had shared the same male partner as her or his own mother, the potential candidate is therefore ineligible to be her or his *axia*.

Taking them altogether, I must confess that I respect the system the Mosuos have worked out for navigating the maze of matrilineal ties that bind a Mosuo family. There is almost a beautiful logic in the way the puzzling pathways eventually join up to reach the end point of the matrilineal heart of the Mosuos.

When in a moment of reflection I take myself on a flight of imagination as an insider within the complex web of Mosuo sensibilities, I find myself uncovering a thousand and one previously unformed thoughts crystallizing into bold reassessments about the intricate network of patrilineal ties that bind a typical Han Chinese family.

As a Mosuo insider looking out into the world of the traditional

Chinese, the first thing that would strike me as incredible is the extent to which Chinese women are debased in society. Much of this shameful attitude still lingers on in rural China.

From the moment a Chinese girl baby is born, she is pushed to the end of the family queue behind her brothers, just because she is a girl. She is not considered an essential part of her father's patrilineal family since his male bloodline only runs through the veins of the boys in the family. The family makes little effort to educate or groom the little girl, especially when she is destined to leave the family to marry and be inducted into her husband's family, at which point most traces of her patrilineal ties with her original family will be erased. From then on she will belong exclusively to the new family she has created with her husband and take on his extended paternal family as her family.

As the new woman, she will quickly learn her place in her husband's patriarchal home. Her fate will be much worse than in her original family. As a wife she will be required to be subservient to her husband, obeying his demands, cooking and looking after him and his family, and bearing children who will never belong to her but to him and his family. As a dutiful daughter-in-law she will be further required to obey her husband's father and mother and tend to their every need and whim. Rarely will she be allowed to escape back to her own family, who at any rate will no longer consider her as part of their family.

To the Mosuo in me, none of this mistreatment of the Chinese woman makes any sense. Any society would have to be crazy to set out deliberately to degrade women in this way. No woman deserves to be so devalued when she is the one who has suffered nine months of pregnancy to give new life to the family. It certainly seems beyond good sense to treat the child born of a woman not as hers or her original family's but as belonging to an outsider family, when the child has been linked naturally to the mother's blood through her umbilical cord. The child is hers from the beginning and should remain so all her life. It is even stranger for the woman's original family to abandon her when she too is inextricably linked to them by her blood.

If the same traditional Chinese woman were to be unlucky enough to land up with a promiscuous husband who takes on mistresses, she will have to suffer the double indignity of recognizing these other women as part of her family and acknowledging the offspring of these women as belonging to her and her husband. Worst of all, only her husband has the right to be polygamous in the patriarchal scheme of things, and if she ever tried to do the same she would do so at the risk of her life.

This patriarchal convention favouring only the man strikes the Mosuo in me as blatantly unfair and illogically unequal. After all, every human person has the same needs and urges, and no society should allow half of its people to enjoy sexual freedom while denying the other half what is natural and good.

If I were to scan across the old, traditional Chinese landscape and find a single mother with a child, I would be shocked to discover that she is treated as the lowest of the low in that society. Without a husband in a marriage to validate her status in society, and without a man to claim paternity over the child, both mother and child would be ostracized from society altogether, with the bastard child growing up ridiculed and shunned all his life.

This shaming of single motherhood in the Chinese world of old would be ludicrous to a Mosuo mind. A female is the only living thing able to give birth to life and every woman is entitled to celebrate child-birth in all its glory. This is the special place reserved for women. A man is never as important as the woman in the act of childbirth. Every woman is a single mother in the sense that she faces child-bearing on her own. Surely it should be incumbent on her family to back the single mother and her child all the way. Life, and particularly new life in a baby, should never be denigrated.

The Chinese patriarchal world may have moved with the times, with some of its rougher edges smoothed over, but many of its old discriminatory attitudes against women still linger on to some degree or another.

While a Chinese woman living in the city today may face fewer male-centric practices, she will still have to contend with some residual one-sided prejudices. If she decides to leave her husband, and many modern Chinese women have divorced in recent times, her main battle will likely be gaining custody of her boy child. She will have to fight against a wall of unadulterated patriarchal defiance that still upholds the dogma of male supremacy. A boy carries his father's bloodline and rightly belongs to the paternal family. The mother has no such right.

My Mosuo response would be outrage, followed by a shrug of my shoulders. A child, whether boy or girl, always belongs to the mother's family, never the man's. No man or his outsider family has the right to wrest away a woman's offspring. Besides which, if the couple had simply chosen a walking marriage instead of a legal marriage in the first place, they would not have to deal with any of the complications of divorce.

A true Mosuo woman could never, and would never, accept all these obvious illogicalities inborn in the mind of the patriarchal Chinese man.

11

The Birth-Death Room

There is a special room in every home in which a Mosuo begins her life at birth and to which she will return at the end of her life to lie in wait for her funeral. It is known appropriately as the 'birth-death room', and is a small stone enclosure tucked at the back of the grandmother's room, which plays out the cycle of life for every Mosuo.

In traditional times, before modern hospitals made their appearance in the villages, a pregnant woman would retreat to the birth-death room to deliver her baby. There she would wait for the big event to come.

No Mosuo woman delivers her baby in this room in the old-fashioned way any more, but I wanted to imagine how it was in those days gone by.

'Is it true that Mosuo women used to squat down to give birth instead of lying down?' I asked Gumi after reading about this somewhere in a book.

'I don't know,' she said. 'I gave birth lying down on the bed, with the help of my mother and a midwife.'

Not getting any help from that quarter, I decided on letting my imagination run with the story of the birth room.

Gumi's heavily pregnant foremother (whom I shall call Dzuoma) was making a simple breakfast by the hearth when her waters broke. She looked up to her mother sitting in her usual position by the grandmother's bed, and raised the alarm. Without wasting a moment, Dzuoma's mother yelled for her other daughter, and together they hustled Dzuoma through the door to the small birth-death room. They let her sit on the bedding, which had been prepared earlier for this eventuality.

Dzuoma sat and groaned as her pains grew more intense. When sweat started to flow down her forehead, the poor girl knew the time was near. She called out to her mother, who came over to help her up into a squatting position. Gritting her teeth, Dzuoma primed herself for the first of a series of pushes to come. Her mother and sister sat on each side of her to hold her steady for the final big effort.

'Push! Push!' Dzuoma's mother coaxed her along. Finally after a long hour, the new grandmother held the small thing in her big hands and shouted elatedly to the rest of the family gathered outside in the courtyard.

'It's a girl!'

A beautiful princess had just entered the world of this humble farmstead and she was delivered without any complications right there inside the little room that had served as the birthing place for generations of this Mosuo family. Swaddled, the newborn was carried by her grandmother out from the birth-death room back to the warmth of the grandmother's room next door.

Later, Dzuoma and her new baby would undergo a period of confinement for a month before relatives, friends and villagers were invited to see and welcome the new addition to Dzuoma's matrilineal family. Everyone stayed to feast at the big welcoming party to celebrate the momentous day and showered Dzuoma with gifts brought from their farms.

The birth-death room had served its purpose for the day and its door would be shut until it was time to welcome its next occupant. This room is seldom used for birthing in modern times and is nowadays utilized solely for its second purpose.

In fact, the first time I ever saw the door to the birth-death room opened was exactly for this reason, when Gumi's mother, A Ma, died. In the last decade or so since her *axia*-turned-husband died, A Ma's health had been failing slowly over time. She would fall seriously ill every now and then, taking to bed, losing her appetite and falling into a silent, listless malaise.

Each time this happened, I would drive myself over to Baju to sit with A Ma for a while. The first time round, I walked into the grandmother's room to see all her eight children with their *axias* assembled there. Gumi as usual fussed over A Ma, feeding her some rice porridge she had cooked over the hearth. Erchima was wiping her brow and mouth and cleaning her hands after she had had her small meal. By the other side of the hearth Zhaxi sat with two of his brothers and reached out to light A Ma the cigarette she was craving even in her discomfort. Outside in the courtyard Jizuo was cutting firewood for the long days ahead.

I found out that each of A Ma's children had dropped everything in order to return home to be with her.

'How long have you been here?' I asked Jizuo.

'The last seven days,' he said.

'Are you staying on?'

'Yes. Until she gets better.'

While there, A Ma's children took turns to comfort her and spent hours sitting by her side. In a lull, they schmoozed about, shooting the breeze to pass the time. Someone cracked a joke, another passed around playing cards to break the monotony. The long vigil nights were punctuated with breaking open the big jar of homemade *kwangtan* brew. When night came, the grown children dozed off one by one on make-shift bedding in A Ma's room.

When I wondered aloud on one of these occasions as to the reason for the entire family gathering by their mother's side, the reply from Zhaxi was short and simple.

'The least we can do as children is to stay with our mother, just in case this is her last journey on earth,' he said.

A Ma's daughters and sons did just that, keeping her company day and night as she grew increasingly frail over the last weeks of her life. They were by her side when she took her last breath. Together her children pulled together their resources to give her a grand send-off.

A Ma's funeral, like all Mosuo ones, is unique. It is one ritual that has not been changed over time, and ranks as the most important sacrament in a person's life. The Mosuos hold dear the funeral rites enacted for the ones who have passed on, especially when they are held in honour of their mother. No expense will be spared for the protracted formalities that can last for as long as weeks or even months.

A Ma was lucky to have had six sons in her large brood of eight children, for only Zhaxi, Jizuo and the other four boys were involved in dealing with the tasks associated with touching A Ma's corpse, from the time of her death all the way to the final cremation, remembering that we are in the land of the Kingdom of Women where Gumi and her older sister, and all the other female relatives, are forbidden to have anything to do with touching death.

All six brothers took up their positions in the grandmother's room, as Zhaxi took the lead in following a ritualized set piece memorialized over the ages. Holding the body of his mother, he began cleaning it before rigor mortis set in, slowly pouring the prescribed number of seven bowls of water over her female face and body. Had it been

Zhaxi's father's funeral, Zhaxi would have used nine bowls.

As he did so, the *daba* stood by to chant the first of many ancient incantations meant to accompany the soul of A Ma from then on until the cremation.

'You are not clean,' sang the *daba*, 'may you be cleansed for the journey back to Sina-Anawah, where your ancestors reside.'

Invoking Sina-Anawah, the *daba* was referring to the Mosuo equivalent of the Garden of Eden. This is a mythical place from where each soul originates and to which the soul returns, waiting to be reincarnated into a new life. Everything connected with a Mosuo funeral revolves around this concept.

As the *daba* continued to chant, Zhaxi, with the help of his brothers, manipulated A Ma's body into a foetal position, in readiness to start a new life in the womb of a new mother. Bending her knees, they moved them close to her face, setting the body in a seated posture. They manoeuvred one of her hands to clasp on to the other and placed them in front of her shins in order to hold the stiffening body in position. Quickly they placed her palms together in a praying gesture and tied a long piece of twine around the body in order to fasten and hold the corpse in this foetus-like pose. Together the sons reverentially lifted the body and placed it in a large linen bag. Zhaxi completed the ritual by fastening the body bag tightly at the top.

At this moment, A Ma's eldest son walked over to open the door to the birth-death room. The other sons moved the body bag through the door into the room and lowered it into a hole dug in the gravel floor. The body was to be left there until the day of the cremation, turning the birth-death room into a temporary tomb for the corpse.

We all waited throughout the afternoon for the other set of holy men from the Tibetan Buddhist monastery to arrive with the pronouncement of the auspicious day for the last rites to be held. The news came with a group of 20 lamas that the day ordained for A Ma's cremation was 17 days away. The Buddhist lamas were deep into their chanting of their sutras in a room lit by dozens of oil lamps next to the grandmother's room when I got back in the evening. As I stepped into the courtyard, the place was abuzz with well-wishers from near and far. I had to squeeze my way through the mourners to get inside the grandmother's room where the nightly ritual was just about to start.

I was taken aback to see that the simple room had been transformed into an unrecognizable funeral parlour. A makeshift platform had been erected next to the Buddhist shrine on which a large but light, square, wooden box had been placed. It was painted with local motifs on a white background.

For a moment I did not recognize it for what it was. Expecting to see a coffin in a familiar long and rectangular shape to accommodate a corpse laid down horizontally, it did not strike me at first that this square, upright chest was a Mosuo coffin. In a flash, it all made sense to me, remembering how A Ma's corpse had been positioned in a seated pose, which would fit into the unusually shaped coffin.

But A Ma's corpse could not have been in the coffin there and then, as she was still interred in the birth-death room. Then it dawned on me that the coffin would remain empty for the duration of the funeral rites until the cremation day.

A Ma was not expected to leave this world without her best ethnic costumes. These were strung up on a pole set above the coffin, ready to be placed inside the coffin with the body just before cremation.

In front of the coffin, a table was set up to serve as the offering altar, on which A Ma's descendants would present three meals, plus *kwang-tan* wine and cigarettes, every day for the duration of the funeral. A Ma should not have to go hungry on her long journey home to Sina-Anawah.

One by one, A Ma's children and grandchildren took turns to kneel and kow-tow in front of the coffin. I saw Gumi and my godchildren go forward to take their turn, praying and weeping in front of the casket. Gumi cried her heart out as she knelt before the symbolic representation of her mother and had to be calmed by two relatives. Ladzu remembered to stretch out her hand to pour wine into a cup set on the table and gestured to the food, inviting the spirit of A Ma to partake of the meal. Collecting herself, Gumi intoned the following words:

'Thank you, A Ma, for looking after us during your lifetime. May you eat well before the long journey to Sina-Anawah. May our family continue to be healthy and to live in peace after your departure.'

As the rest of the family queued to take their places, the *daba* standing by the coffin started chanting a hauntingly mournful tune in a minor key, using the same sad melody to recite from a piece of paper in his hand the full names of each and every member of A Ma's family. It took an eternity for him to finish naming all her relatives, but afterwards he went on chanting the ancient *daba* invocations.

'My task at a funeral is to open the way for the dead person's soul, so that it can travel all the way back to Sina-Anawah,' a *daba* said to me on a previous occasion when I managed to draw out from him the most interesting explanation of the shamanistic rituals conducted for a funeral.

'The words I chant will lead the way for the soul to return to the place where we Mosuos originally came from. I chant the words to guide the way and to warn the soul of the possible dangers and perils along the journey. I tell the soul not to be afraid, as the road to Sina-Anawah may be difficult and treacherous. I say to the soul that it may run into the path of savage animals and menacing evil spirits on the way. I will chant of ways to help the soul avoid these dangers. Then I tell the soul that after it reaches Sina-Anawah, it will find a new life and return among the living, able once again to help her or his family.'

Outside, neighbours and friends crowded around. Volunteers from A Ma's large circle of friends served up dinner, a community effort assembled from dishes prepared by different households in the village.

The scene on that first night of A Ma's funeral was repeated every night for more than a fortnight until the eve of the cremation. The penultimate night was the culmination of the mourning period and, according to Mosuo beliefs, was the moment the soul had reached the last and most treacherous leg of its passage back to the ancient spiritual land of Sina-Anawah.

To help A Ma's soul to overcome the dangers looming before her, the *daba* took centre stage in the courtyard outside to play out an extraordinary shamanistic ritual aimed at guiding the departing soul along.

Appearing in the same colourful, traditional shamanic outfit since the morning, the *daba* signalled to a waiting group of male relatives and friends to approach him. The first pair stepped forward. The *daba* helped each of them put on ancient-looking leather armour and feathered headgear before handing them a couple of old swords and daggers. Now dressed like two warriors from the past, the pair acted out a fiendish dance routine round the courtyard, chasing invisible spirits while shouting battle cries, brandishing their swords in a mock fight against unseen wild animals, and clearing the way for the soul on its last lap home.

When the first pair finished their act, another two volunteers went up to take their places, donning the same outfits and performing the same ritual. Round and round the different pairs of 'warriors' put on more of the mock-menacing routine to terrify the evils lurking in the night. The hour-long stunning spectacle of the age-old dance of the funereal bodyguards was a reminder to me of how dear the Mosuos hold their pagan customs in their hearts.

The frenetic activity going on in the courtyard was counterpoised by the more sedate chanting of the Buddhist lamas in their saffron- and burgundy-coloured robes seated inside. An equally crucial part of every Mosuo funeral, the holy men of the Buddha continued with their invocations to help deliver the soul of the recently departed A Ma towards reincarnation. On hearing the riotous crowd outside, I distinctly discerned the group-chant droning on louder and louder in the background. I peeked through the doorway and saw the large group of seated lamas making an effort to ratchet up their chorus, possibly in a show of one-upmanship against the *daba*'s performance.

I marvelled at the picture before me, the two faiths competing with each other in rendering their respective versions of the final send-off and yet co-existing side by side on this sad night. It spoke volumes for the low-key tolerance and understanding shown by both sides of the local religious divide. Yet there was no divide, because the ambivalent nature of the Mosuos has adopted the relatively new Buddhist religion without letting go of their pagan past. Every Mosuo family makes sure to include both religious expressions in each funeral.

Exhausted and grimy, since Mosuos do not allow themselves to bathe or cut their hair throughout the mourning period, the relatives stayed up one last night in the final wake to keep company with the departing soul. Night vigil turned into daylight energy, as everyone got ready to play his part in the final rite when dawn broke.

A day before this cremation morning, the menfolk had erected a small replica log home at the cremation site, chosen at the base of a hill behind A Ma's village. Miniaturized to fit the coffin, the log structure resembled a typical Mosuo home erected with interlocking pine logs. As this was the funeral of a woman, her replica home was seven logs high. If the funeral had been for a man, his replica home would be nine logs high.

Back at home, one of Gumi's brothers designated himself as the horse-handler of the day and had already dressed the lead pony. Both pony and handler waited in front of the house to head the funeral procession in due time.

Tension built up as the men laid out a long length of white cloth from the front door across the courtyard all the way to the front gate of the house.

It was time.

Inside grandmother's room and in private, shielded by a portable cloth screen, A Ma's sons made their way to the door of the birth-death room. Together they walked in to carry the now-leaking body bag into the grandmother's room. Solemnly they lifted the body bag into the square coffin, added A Ma's clothing and placed the coffin cover on top.

Lining up in twin rows, the son pallbearers hoisted the poles holding the coffin on to their shoulders. Slowly they bore the coffin out of the house to face a newly formed line of women and children who had taken position to kneel along the white cloth in the courtyard. The men carefully manoeuvred the coffin right across and over the prostrated heads of the kneeling relatives. As they moved over the heads of the mourners, an extraordinarily moving sight ensued. Every one of those kneeling started to cry and weep, wailing her own farewell to the departing A Ma in her coffin.

The procession then moved towards the gate. The son horse-handler pulled on the reins and walked the horse to lead the pallbearers out of the door. Loud firecrackers started firing ahead, followed by sounds of a gong being beaten. Carried aloft, the coffin tracked the pony, followed by a long line of mourners who had taken up the rear after rising from their kneeling positions. More firecrackers were set off ahead of the cortege, chasing evil spirits away.

Swiftly the group ascended the hillside to arrive at the cremation site. The male pallbearers set the coffin down next to the replica log structure. In one swift move shielded from the eyes of the women and children by a handheld wooden screen, they hoisted the body bag out of the coffin and placed it inside the replica home. The pallbearers broke the emptied coffin into pieces and added them into the last resting place of A Ma.

Facing A Ma in her funeral pyre, Gumi and the rest of the women and child mourners prostrated themselves on the rough earth and began weeping and wailing their goodbyes one last time, while the male mourners stood stoically on the side with their heads bowed. All kow-towed to the deceased for the final time.

By the side, the lamas seated in two rows started the send-off chants, ringing tiny bells and sprinkling holy water. As their characteristic sonorous bass voices sounded the final chorus, a junior monk lit a long-handled ladle of yak butter oil and sprinted to the log structure to set it alight. The first flames caught quickly, lighting up the funeral pyre. The lighting of the fire was the signal the Mosuos believed to be the exact moment the soul of A Ma was released from its bodily form, to fly on its way to a new reincarnation.

At this point, the send-off was over. The goodbyes were done, the crying was over, and nothing more was left. There was no need to tarry any longer. It was now time for the female relatives to turn their backs on this their once beloved. Just as quickly, Gumi and all the women and children stood up to go. It was time to leave A Ma now that she had left on her final journey to Sina-Anawah.

I stayed behind to watch the lamas chanting the final prayers as the funeral fire burned on. The men too stayed on, waiting for the embers to die down before cleaning up the funeral site.

There was one last ritual. A Ma's sons returned the following morning to collect her ashes. The six of them walked up the hill to strew them to the wind.

12

On the Knife-Edge
of Extinction

Curiosity led me to Gemu Mountain Goddess and the festival in her honour, serendipity invited me to live half of the time in my Mosuo home, but it was the magic of the extraordinary Mosuo people of Lugu Lake that initiated me into the feminist utopia of the Kingdom of Women.

In this place of another time and humanity, I have come round to finding a new feminism within me. My journey has been an unexpectedly life-changing experience, and even as I have changed I sense great change coming for the matrilineal Mosuos as they march in step with contemporary China.

The Mosuo stories I have collected and grown to love are born of another time when Mother Earth was new. They speak of a time of simplicity and a time of naivety in the best sense of the word. It was a time when early humans made the best of what Mother Nature provided and gave thanks to what they understood to be the symbol of the original life force, the female. In looking for a higher being having protective power from on high, the Mosuos put a female face to the most magnificent physical structure in their land and called her Gemu

Mountain Goddess. With Gemu looking over their everyday lives, the Mosuos chose the simplest form of organizing themselves, tracing everything to mother and all that comes with motherliness.

For all that, Mosuo simplicity and naivety have no place in the twenty-first century. The very lives of the people in this Garden of Eden are evolving as fast as modernity is marching into their world. In the blink of an eye, in the six years I have lived among this community, I have borne witness at first hand to how quickly they have moved from their subsistence-farming way of life to plug right into the new world as cogs in the burgeoning tourism machinery of China. Almost overnight every aspect of their traditional lives is being tested against the mores and values of a new, alternative society.

With modern times come modern, alternative ways of looking at life. The Mosuos can no longer insulate themselves from these new-fangled ideas permeating through the schools, television, smart phones and increasing contact with tourists from the outside world. With modernization the old insular way of life in the Kingdom of Women is seriously under threat of losing out to the prevailing patriarchal culture of the Chinese. In the process the Mosuos are slowly losing steam in keeping safe their ancestral matrilineal roots.

The change started a couple of decades ago when provincial authorities were looking at promising sites for tourism in Yunnan. Lugu Lake, hitherto closed to outsiders, fitted the bill, with its pristine mountain scenery and an interesting socio-anthropological story to boot.

Before tourism, before the trickle of solo backpackers and way before the bus loads of gawking tourists, the Mosuo people had been eking out a hand-to-mouth living, tilling the land, rearing a handful of farm animals, gathering the meagre offerings of the forest and hunting the occasional wild hog and pheasant. Life was simple then.

Change sneaked into their world. Previously inaccessible other than by a trek through virgin pine forests, Lugu Lake saw its first mountain path hewn from rocky cliff sides in the 1990s, linking it to the major regional township of Lijiang, itself a phoenix rebuilt from the ashes caused by a massive earthquake in 1996.

A few adventurous travellers hitchhiked on trucks, making their way to this isolated region. They came whispering tales of the outside world, of a world where water came out of a tap on demand instead of being hauled in from a well, and where at the touch of a switch the grandmother's room would be lit up without having to burn a splinter of pine wood. And wonder of wonders, the villagers saw visitors arriving on self-propelled motorbikes and cars not drawn by horses.

Time passed, and with it came the realization by the local authorities of the tourism potential of this rustic and scenic goldmine. To kick-start the industry, they sold the idea of a tribe still locked in their world of free love and sex and threw open the door to the Mosuo world. They upgraded the mountain path to a tarmac road, which was the road I took when I made my first seven-hour journey into the Kingdom of Women.

Six years on, I drive through a modern two-lane highway complete with tunnels blasted through the mountain ridges, cutting my travel time to five hours. Tour buses now pick up travellers from the spanking-new airport at Lugu Lake, adding hundreds more tourists to those arriving by bus on a daily basis. A new super-highway opening soon will establish the once sleepy hollow of Lugu Lake as one of the top visitor destinations in China.

Tourists leave behind in their wake a detritus of totally foreign and challenging ideas, such as the cash economy, mass consumerism and the male-dominant Chinese culture. Likewise the Mosuo agrarian-based barter economy has suddenly been catapulted into a world where cash is king. In a short decade or so, locals have slowly but surely discovered that cash allows them access to many things they never had before or thought they needed. Those villagers who had grown up toiling bare-foot in the fields and making do with whatever the land provided or the hand crafted, are now tempted by an endless array of consumer goods.

In these modern times, people aspire to buy new status symbols. Owning a washing machine is a mark that a Mosuo household has arrived. So are flushing toilets and solar-powered hot-water showers. Owning a motorbike or, better still, a four-wheel drive is *de rigueur* for a man. Not content with simply owning a mobile phone, villagers compare each other's smart phones, with the cash-richer ones showing off their latest iPhone or Samsung models.

The rapid change from an ancient agrarian life to a millennium lifestyle touches not only the material things in life but also the old customs and values. I see it everywhere I turn.

The native ensemble, a jacket cinched over a long, circular skirt, is packed away in a young woman's cupboard nowadays.

'I only wear it on special occasions, or when I dance in the bonfire dance for the tourists,' a young friend explained.

She is more regularly seen in a pair of trendy tight jeans topped with a snug leather jacket, Hollywood style. Her mother, in her 40s, similarly eschews her native dress, preferring the modern Chinese style of a pair of pants with a top. Only her grandmother, in her 60s, goes about her daily life wearing the ethnic long-skirted costume.

Birthday celebrations, or the lack thereof, are another example. The concept of celebrating one's birthday is alien to the Mosuos for the reason that a mother's birthing pains are not a cause for celebration.

'How do you count your age then?' I asked Jizuo.

'Well, like everybody else, I know I am one year older when the Spring Festival comes along,' he said.

On the other hand, his daughter Ercher, the mother of my new goddaughter who has set up home with her *axia*, has decided to follow the new practice of celebrating her toddler's birthday. The doting parents, both in their 20s, belong to the generation fed on a television diet of Chinese people marking their children's birthdays. To keep up with the Xis and the Maos, they follow suit. Come every 8 February – yes, the parents even remember the actual date he was born – they buy him a birthday cake from the town's only baker and invite all the young cousins of the boy to watch him blow out the candles. I suspect the young parents feel they are rather cool when they do this.

More than washing machines and birthday cakes, villagers have keyed in to the value of their farmland. Poor local farmers have become rich landlords overnight, renting their small plots to Chinese investors from the cities to build hotels, restaurants and holiday resorts by Lugu Lake. The more savvy among the locals have joined in the rush to buy up land from eager sellers ready to make a quick buck from their farm plots.

With spare cash and more leisure time than ever before, the erstwhile peasants now turned lessors are forever in search of a good time. Hunting has been replaced by new and modern pastimes. The Mosuos have taken to feasting, drinking, gambling and drugging in a big way. Many of my friends now sit at mahjong tables or card games to while away their time – and cash. More and more of the younger set I know are experimenting with hard drugs like opium and heroin. A few of them are sitting in jail for trafficking offences.

The relentless onslaught of the cash economy has seen a rapid change in the lives of those inhabiting the tourist hotspots right beside the lake. This is especially evident in the hamlet of Lige which commands the most beautiful spot by Lugu Lake and therefore accommodates the highest number of tourists among the many small communities dotted all round the inland sea. It used to be an extremely poor village, its infertile soil not good enough for grain, sustaining only the most simple crops like corn and potatoes. Today the former lakefront farm properties host dozens of restaurants and hotels.

Young people are rushing after the many jobs opening up in the belly of the cash cow. Whereas youngsters could once only look forward to a life of tilling the land, they now enter the tourist workforce as drivers, hotel and restaurant staff and small-time entrepreneurs running modest eateries and barbeque stands. They are filling their pockets with wages that have trebled in the short time I have been there.

To my great disappointment, my godson Nongbu set his sights on joining this increasing band of young people wanting to earn a quick buck. From a sweet, gallant young boy when I first met him, Nongbu became a pugnacious lad of 16, too self-important to listen to anyone when he made the decision to quit his junior high schooling on a whim.

No amount of persuasion on his parents' and my part to change his mind had any effect after he dropped the bombshell on us.

'Finishing your schooling is very important for your future,' I said to him.

'I am never going back to school,' he maintained.

'What are you going to do then?'

'I am going to work as a waiter in Zhaxi Guesthouse. Later I will open my own barbeque stand, or maybe I will join the army.'

I was devastated. It was only much later that I came to accept that Nongbu had few role models to follow. He could either be a woodcutter like his father or take after his two male cousin brothers, both of whom had left school early with one becoming a waiter and the other a sous chef in Lige. This was Nongbu's world, as seen from his adolescent perspective. It was a sign of the times and of the peer pressures youngsters face in this fast-developing region.

The experience in Lige is a telling example of how modern life is beginning to impinge on the old community spirit of the Mosuos. Community leaders are so concerned about the falling numbers of villagers willing to help at community events that they have had to resort to a most un-Mosuo attempt to keep the old ways alive. They are imposing hefty fines on those households that fail to participate. Out of compulsion, but also shamed into submission, the Lige villagers now show up at community events. At a recent funeral wake, I counted over 40 friends and acquaintances busying themselves, the women cooking and serving up food for the crowds who came to pay their respects, and the men clearing up the mess afterwards. The disincentive seemed to work, at least for the present.

The onslaught from the modern Chinese economy has reached as far as Gumi's village deep inside the Mosuo farmlands. Someone has started a large commercial mushroom farm on land that was previously given over to corn and rice. The company running the business rents multiple small plots in the vicinity from villagers willing to give up their subsistence farming in exchange for cash in hand.

In an effort to stem the tide, I started a social enterprise to encourage the people of Baju to continue growing the delicious and nutritious highland red rice grown in these parts. The idea was a simple one.

If I could buy a sufficient quantity of the special red rice at a premium to be paid on a fair-trade basis to make commercial sense, I could sell it as a boutique health product at a much higher retail price. The premium paid to the farmers would go some way to sustaining local rice farming on an ongoing basis while the profit generated could be ploughed back to fund worthwhile community projects in the area.

Serendipity hit again when I had a chance reunion with an old college-mate, Ben, who happened to have been in the food business in China since graduation. Ben graduated from McGill University in Canada in agricultural science. I casually told him the story of my proposed rice project.

'Do you have any ideas about marketing the highland red rice from small farmers in the Kingdom of Women?' I ventured to ask.

'Why, that is a good idea, especially if it is for a charitable purpose,' he said enthusiastically. 'You know I run a food and beverage business. I can use my contacts in Beijing to sell however much you can assemble from the farmers.'

That two-liner conversation started my social-enterprise project, which is now in its second year of operation. But sustaining the traditional rice farming of the Baju villagers is admittedly a small step on the way to halting the gradual erosion of traditional life. There are bigger dangers looming ahead for the Mosuo community.

Not forgetting the waning interest in keeping alive the only ethnic festival of Gemu worth preserving, even the unique institution of walking marriage is under threat. Nowadays more and more young sexual partners turn their backs on the *sese* tradition. I decided to explore the phenomenon by engaging university graduate Xiaomei, the younger daughter of Jizuo, in a conversation about her future life plans.

'Do you have a boyfriend?' I asked.

'No, not yet.'

'Do you think you will practise *sese* or get married?'

'I will most certainly get married. I do not believe walking marriage is the right way to start a family. Anyway, I don't think I will marry a Mosuo man. Mosuo men are not good in the way they go about having different *axias* all the time.'

Here in a nutshell is the story of a changing attitude among young Mosuos who are fully educated and integrated into the modern Chinese system of nuclear families and all its attendant patriarchal values.

I recently received a wedding invitation from a young Mosuo couple who started out as a *sese* couple not long ago. I remember driving them back to the remote village home of the young woman so that he could meet her family for the first time. It was romantic for the 18-year-old girl to introduce her *axia* to all the members of her matrilineal family. I was taken aback when they told me they were getting married.

'Why are you getting married when you are both Mosuos?' I asked what must have been an impolite question.

'Oh, it's much nicer this way,' the young man said.

'It's better to go through a marriage these days,' the young woman piped up, nodding in agreement.

Theirs is not the only wedding between Mosuo couples I have attended in the last couple of years, each one of them grander than the last. Some of them take the plunge on a common-law basis without actually registering the marriage, but more go the whole legal route, signing official marriage papers before the civil authorities.

Invariably the new husband and wife leave their respective matrilineal households to build their one-man-one-woman home and bring up their children as a couple. They go on to teach their child to call her father 'Papa', following the Chinese custom. This child will not grow up using the old Mosuo term 'Abu' to denote the more distant parental relationship of a Mosuo man to his child.

Yet for some who have turned their backs on the *sese* society, the old habit dies hard. A capable, young *axia*-about-town I know is currently in his third marriage after two relatively short-lived legal liaisons. During his first marriage, he must have found he was ill suited to the demands of monogamy. On discovering he had reverted back to his *axia* lifestyle, his first Mosuo wife immediately demanded a divorce, as well as an expensive settlement allowed by the civil court.

Not one to be deterred, he married a second time. Again, he could not give up his old ways, with the second wife demanding an equally costly divorce settlement. Now for the third time, he is attempting to live up to the modern expectations of fidelity never required by his previous *sese* relationships. Perhaps he will finally find the mettle to fit the mould of a good Chinese husband.

In these changing times, the Mosuo man is increasingly being challenged to remodel the traditional role familiar to his forefathers. He may have to give up his carefree ways and act responsibly as a husband to his wife and as a father to his children if he is to follow the new norm of being a Chinese man.

The Mosuo woman has her own challenges that go with modern mores incumbent on being a good Chinese woman. A close woman friend of mine recounted to me a testy conversation she had with her niece after hearing stories of the young girl going with a couple of *axias*.

'I told her not to be so stupid. I said to her that no man would marry her if word got around that she was going to bed with everyone she met,' she said.

This coming from a middle-aged Mosuo woman who has led a walking-marriage lifestyle was striking on many levels. In one stroke she repudiated the institution of *sese* and bought wholesale into the value system of Chinese patriarchy so foreign to the Mosuo mindset.

More threatening is the possibility of the matrilineal family disintegrating over time. In its previous incarnation, the large three-generational matrilineal family was an efficient production unit, with its many hands making light work of farming, gathering and hunting. Without question, the fruits of their joint labour were shared equally among all the family members. Modern jobs bring in different incomes, with the more productive members of the family being loath to share their money with the less productive ones. Better to split the family land into as many plots as there are siblings so as to give each her or his own spoils.

Like so many Mosuo families adjusting to the new realities thrown up by the cash economy, the Aha family after the death of the grandmother is in the process of splitting up into separate households headed by each of her children. The Aha matrilineal family I grew to be fond of will no longer exist in time to come.

From a traditionalist perspective it is clear that the old ways are in their death throes, slowly but relentlessly. To me it is clear that the Mosuos are at a crossroads, with each young person wondering whether to continue down the well-trodden matrilineal path or traverse what to them is a new and exciting but patrilineal road. As more of the young veer off course, the old values are disappearing. Nowadays I have to travel further inland to the more remote and cut-off hamlets to find authentic matrilineal families who still live true to their ancestral values.

Whether the Kingdom of Women is teetering on the knife-edge of extinction remains to be seen. I suspect no one can predict how long the Mosuos will hold out in these times of change. But I do take comfort from the reflection that the last thing that will survive will be their core belief in the matrilineal principle. They may compromise on the more peripheral issues such as their traditional dress, birthdays, marriage, nuclear family units and divorce, but I dare to think that the thread that endures, the last thing that will disappear, will be their maternal bloodlines.

More age-old customs will surely break down in these modern times, and the Mosuo cosmos that I have come to know and respect may well be a thing of the past. I am just glad to have caught it in transition.

Glossary

a ma	The Mosuo term for mother.
abu	The Mosuo word for father.
Ah Shang	A male mountain god.
amur	The Mosuo word for older sister or brother.
axia	The Mosuo word for lover, of either gender.
Baju	The hamlet where the author's godchildren live.
Baoshan	A regional township in Yunnan.
chuoduo	The Mosuo word for the stone platform in front of the hearth, the place to make offerings of food to the matrilineal ancestors.
daba	A male shaman in the old Mosuo pagan tradition.
Dali	A tourist destination in the province of Yunnan.
Duojie	A Tibetan Buddhist priest who is a friend of the author.
Ercher	The elder daughter of Jizuo and the young mother of my newest goddaughter.
Ercher Dzuoma	The local name of the author chosen by the Living Buddha of Yongning.

Erchima	A close woman friend of the author.
ganma	The Chinese word for godmother.
Gelupa	The Yellow Hat sect of Tibetan Buddhism.
Gemu	The Mountain Goddess, the patron female deity of the Mosuo people.
gepie sese	The Mosuo term for an open, conspicuous relationship between a woman and a man in their 'walking marriage' tradition.
gizi	The Mosuo word for younger brother.
gumi	The Mosuo word for younger sister.
hadaq	The long white, yellow or red scarf used by Tibetan Buddhists as a blessing to be conferred on a recipient.
Han or Han Chinese	The dominant ethnic group in China, a term originally derived from the Han Dynasty (206BC–220AD) and used to describe mainstream Chinese people and culture.
ji the ti dzi	The Mosuo term for an adoption-cohabitation relationship between a woman and a man in the 'walking marriage' tradition.
jiachuo	The Mosuo circle dance round a bonfire.
Jinshajiang	The Chinese term for the Golden Sand Stream, a tributary of the Yangtze River.
Jizuo	The sixth brother of Gumi, also a friend of the author.
Kingdom of Women	Also known as the Kingdom of Daughters, the name given to the villages and hamlets by Lugu Lake inhabited by the matrilineal Mosuos.
Kunming	The provincial capital of Yunnan.

kwangtan	The Chinese name for a home-brewed wine, meaning to collapse and fall over after drinking the heady stuff.
Ladzu	The author's Mosuo goddaughter.
lama	A Tibetan Buddhist priest.
Lige	Hamlet on the shore of Lugu Lake, a well-known tourist destination.
Lugu Lake	A lake straddling the provinces of Yunnan and Sichuan.
Luoshui	A big Mosuo village by Lugu Lake.
mabang	Literally a 'horse-helper' in Chinese, a stable-hand.
Majang Ah Hong	Nickname of the author, meaning Ah Hong who lives on the horse farm.
Moon Lake	Also known as the Middle Sea, the small lake at the foot of Gemu Goddess Mountain beside the author's Mosuo home.
Mosuo	Name of the tribe of people living by Lugu Lake, who are matrilineal by descent and who speak a Burmese-Tibetan language.
mou	A Chinese measurement of an area of land.
Na	The original name of the Mosuo tribe in the Mosuo language.
nana sese	The Mosuo term for a furtive, secretive relationship between a woman and a man in the 'walking marriage' tradition.
Nongbu	The author's Mosuo godson.
Puna	A male mountain god.
ri-cher	The Mosuo phrase for 'cheers' or 'bottoms up'.
RMB	The Chinese currency, *renminbi*, also known as the yuan.

Sakya	The Red Hat sect of Tibetan Buddhism.
sese	The Mosuo word for the way their love life is conducted, with the man 'walking' to or 'visiting' his *axia*'s home to spend the night together and leaving at dawn to return to his own home.
song rong	A pine mushroom, also known as *matsutake*.
ti dzi ji mao the	The Mosuo term for a cohabitation relationship between a woman and a man in the 'walking marriage' tradition.
visiting marriage	Same as walking marriage.
walking marriage	The Mosuo practice of a man visiting his lover at her home but returning to his own home in the morning.
Xiaomei	The younger daughter of Jizuo and the first university graduate in Gumi's family.
Xiao Wujing	The competitive swimmer daughter of Erchima and Zhaxi.
Xiao Zhaxi	Little Zhaxi, the son of Erchima and Zhaxi.
Xienami	The Mosuo name for Lugu Lake.
Yongning	A major town by Lugu Lake, centre of the matrilineal Mosuo tribe.
yuan	The Chinese currency, the same as the *renminbi*.
Yunnan	A province of south-west China.
Zhamei Si	The Gelupa Tibetan Buddhist temple in Yongning.
Zhaxi	Gumi's seventh sibling and the builder of the author's home by Moon Lake.
Zhuanshanjie	The festival to celebrate Gemu Mountain Goddess on the 25th day of the seventh month in the lunar calendar; in Chinese it means perambulating round the mountain.